OKINAWAN GOJU-RYU
THE FUNDAMENTALS OF SHOREI-KAN KARATE

GASHO, where the hands are pressed together in front of the solar plexus, and LOTUS, where the legs are crossed, form the classic position for Zen meditation. The karate techniques and movements explained in this text evolved from this position.

OKINAWAN GOJU-RYU
THE FUNDAMENTALS OF SHOREI-KAN KARATE
BY
SEIKICHI TOGUCHI

Compiled by Toshio Tamano

GRAPHIC DESIGN BY DAVID PAUL KAPLAN

©Ohara Publications, Incorporated 1976
All rights reserved
Printed in the United States of America
Library of Congress Catalog Card Number: 75-36054

Seventeenth printing 2000

ISBN 0-89750-018-0

OHARA Ⓟ PUBLICATIONS, INCORPORATED
SANTA CLARITA, CALIFORNIA

ACKNOWLEDGEMENTS

I wish to express my sincerest and deepest thanks to Toshio Tamano for his perseverance and dedication in the design, translation and editing of my work and for his supreme effort in helping me see it to completion; to Aris Kyriazoglou for his excellent photographic services; to Ichiro Naito and Mr. Tamano for their time in posing for the hundreds of forms required; to Sherry Gordon, Peter Seaton and Mr. Naito for their assistance in translating this work from Japanese to English; to all the students of Shorei-Kan Karate who supported me and assisted me in every phase of the execution of this book.

Seikichi Toguchi

DEDICATION

To Master Chojun Miyagi for his guidance and great effort in the creation of *Goju-Ryu Karate.*

ABOUT THE AUTHOR

Born on May 20, 1917, in Naha City, Okinawa, Seikichi Toguchi studied karate under Master Chojun Miyagi and his assistant, Mr. Seko Higa. During World War II, Mr. Toguchi served the Japanese Imperial Army as an electrical engineer in Southeast Asia. He returned to Okinawa in 1946 to find the land barren and devastated, the people starving and depressed. Recognizing his homeland's need for vital reconstruction, he devoted himself to rebuilding Okinawa. When a new dojo was finally established from out of the rubble, the Okinawan Athletic Association offered him a teaching position. He accepted their offer and taught for two years in what was then the only karate dojo in all post-war Okinawa.

When, in 1952, Master Miyagi organized the Goju-Ryu Association to oversee the establishment and maintenance of the Goju-Ryu style, Mr. Toguchi was named its executive director. Two years later, the Goju-Ryu Association became the Goju-Kai Federation and Mr. Toguchi was elected vice-president.

Among his other honors, Mr. Toguchi includes the Japan Karate Federation's invitation to participate as the Okinawan master at their first opening demonstration and his participation in the first world karate tournament held in Tokyo in 1969.

At present, Mr. Toguchi divides his time between teaching at his schools in Tokyo and Koza City.

PREFACE

Karate, which originated in Okinawa, today enjoys world-wide popularity. This is reflected in the many books written on the subject and their volume of sales. These books, however, while dealing with an art of Okinawan origin, are written by karate men from places other than the Ryukyu Islands. Considering the abundance of their material, it is difficult to understand why a karate textbook written by an Okinawan master himself has never been published. There exists no literature or reference source on the techniques of the Okinawan masters, written by them. Foreign karateka, visiting the islands to further their studies, must grope for information because there is no textbook to help them organize and assimilate these techniques. The intent herein is to present (hopefully without pretension) such a textbook.

A complex art, karate demands great discipline and dedication. As a result, it must be learned gradually and progressively. Teaching beginners difficult classic kata such as *passai* or *seisan* is comparable to teaching elementary school boys college level subjects. Similarly, emphasizing free-fighting competition to novices is sending an untrained army into battle. Students must move from basics to complexities in a prescribed manner. To facilitate this progression and simplify the study of karate, I have developed *Hookiyu Kata* (Unified Kata), a unified system of learning for beginning students of *Goju-Ryu Shorei-Kan Karate*. A combination of styles, though predominantly Okinawan, it provides a basic training for the pupil and gives him background necessary for both classic kata and fighting competition.

I feel great responsibility in my mission as an Okinawan master. Therefore, I present this textbook to introduce *Hookiyu Kata* and to uphold the true spirit of the traditional Okinawan Karate-Do Goju Ryu style.

CONTENTS

HISTORY 12
    Karate's Mission and Aim 12
    History of Okinawan Karate-Do 12
    The Development of Modern Karate-Do 13
    The Origin of Goju-Ryu 14
    Master Kanryo Higashionna 14
    Master Chojun Miyagi 15
HOOKIYU KATA 18
    Necessity of Unified Kata and its Meaning 18
    Merits of Unified Kata 19
    The Curriculum and its Combination 19
    Ranking System and Curriculum 21
    Hookiyu Kata Subjects 21
BASICS 25
    Enbusen Diagram 26
    Foot Scale 26
    Fist Scale 26
    Musubidachi Stance 27
    Heikodachi Stance 28
    Kihondachi Stance 29
    Basic Walking 30
    Zenkutsu Dachi Stance 31
    Sho (Small) Zenkutsu Dachi Stance 32
    Shikodachi Stance 33
    Renoji Dachi Stance 34
    Hachiji Dachi Stance 35
    How to Make the Seiken Fist 36
    How to Use the Seiken Fist 38
    Kamae or Basic On-Guard Position 39
    Beginning Formality 40
    Ending Formality 42
    Chudan Tsuki (Middle Punch) 44
    Jodan Tsuki (High Punch) 46
    Gedan Tsuki (Low Punch) 47
    Chudan Uke (Middle Block) 48
    Jodan Uke (High Block) 50
    Gedan Uke (Low Block) 52
HOOKIYU KATA NO. 1 AND ITS BUNKAI 55
    Morote Tsuki (Double Punch) 56

Suihei Shuto Uchi (Side Chop) 58
How to Read the Diagrams 59
Kata and Bunkai 60
KISO KUMITE NO. 1 81
Yoko Kentsui Uchi (Hammer Punch to the Temple) . . . 82
Age Tsuki (Upper Cut) 84
Set I 86
Set II 88
Set III 90
Set IV 92
Set V 94
Set VI 96
KISO KUMITE NO. 2 99
Mae Shuto Uchi (Front Chop Strike) 100
Soko Tsuki (Under Cut) 102
Set I 104
Set II 106
Set III 108
Set IV 110
Set V 112
Set VI 114
GEKISAI NO. 1 KATA AND BUNKAI 117
Shomen Geri (Front Kick) 118
Tate Empi (Elbow Attack) 120
Shomen Geri/Tate Empi (Front Kick/
    Elbow Attack) Combination 122
Shomen Geri/Tate Empi Combination
    Blocking Sequence 124
Uraken Uchi (Back Fist Strike) 126
Kata and Bunkai 128
SANCHIN 159
Zen and Sanchin 160
Sanchin Training Method 161
Sanchin Walking 162
The Five Techniques in the Breathing Method 164
Symbols for Sanchin Breathing 165
Clarification of Techniques Used in Nos. 6-46 . . . 166
Clarification of Techniques Used in Nos. 47-54 . . . 168
Sanchin Exercise 170
GLOSSARY 191

HISTORY

KARATE'S MISSION and AIM

Karate was born when peace, the heart of the Okinawan people, was incorporated with the spirit of Zen as embodied in Chinese Shorin Temple boxing. Its aim, therefore, is completely different from any other martial art. Whereas the chief aim of all other martial arts is killing and wounding as many opponents as possible, karate's primary concern is simply self-defense. Of course, defense and offense cannot exist without each other. Consequently, training in superior defensive techniques necessitates training in superior offensive techniques.

Now, the growing interest in karate results not from the excellence of its technique or the Oriental mystique; rather, this interest stems from an ever-increasing appreciation for the spirit of Zen Buddhism and the Okinawan spirit of peace. It is this author's fervent hope that the spirit of Karate-Do presented in this book will be understood and peace will come to the world through an appreciation of this spirit.

HISTORY of OKINAWAN KARATE-DO

Okinawa, an island country with few natural resources to support its large population, has historically imposed great physical and political hardship on its inhabitants. In spite of this, the people maintained an indomitable will to survive. When unprovoked persecution and hostility greeted them, these basically peace-loving people drew on their inherent martial arts spirit. They then fought weaponless against armed opponents, using only their bare hands in a self-defense method called *karate-jutsu*. Their hands and feet, normally occupied with non-violent activities, became, in themselves, weapons through the use of these techniques. The technique called *shuto* (chop), still in use today, is a vestige of those early times when hands first functioned as swords.

Though much of their defense was unarmed, the Okinawans occasionally used weapons against armed opponents. These weapons included the *nunchaku*, a neck of stringed instruments used as a wooden sword, and reels which were thrown as missiles. Perhaps the prohibition of weapons by Lord Shoshin in 1488 and the famous battle of Keicho in 1609 were factors in the development of these karate weapons. In the battle of Keicho, the people of Shuri City, lacking weapons utilized instruments of daily life. The *nunchaku* began as a horse bridle or wagon shaft, *tonfa* came from a potato digger or crop grinder, and *timbei* came from a pot cover.

Some have argued that development of Okinawan karate techniques resulted from the use of these weapons, particularly at the battle of Keicho. This, however, was not the case. Karate techniques facilitated use of these weapons, not vice versa, and presupposed their utilization at the battle of Keicho. In fact, deprivation of the right to bear arms stimulated the development of karate-do in Okinawa.

THE DEVELOPMENT of MODERN KARATE-DO

In the beginning, karate was simply called *tee* (hand). When, in the late 1800's, *tee* was incorporated in Okinawan junior high school physical training programs, it was given the name *karate* (empty hand) to distinguish it from *todee* (Chinese hand), a form of *tee* introduced from China. Literally, karate means "bare hands and naked fists."

The two original styles of karate, developed in the regions of Shuri-Tomari and Naha, were called *Shuri-te* and *Naha-te*, respectively. Many karate masters contributed to these styles but the two considered the fathers of modern karate are Master Anko Itosu of *Shuri-te* and Master Kanryo Higashionna of *Naha-te*. They are often called the matchless twin-stars. In the early 1900's, Master Itosu introduced and taught karate as a regular course in the physical education programs of Naha normal and junior high schools. Master Higashionna did the same in the police schools and other junior high schools in Naha. In this manner, they carried karate from the fighting methods of the past to its modern stature as a martial art. The *Shuri-te* style of Master Itosu eventually became *Shorin-Ryu*, while Master Higashionna, using *Shuri-te* as his point of departure, eventually developed *Naha-te*, the predecessor of today's *Goju-Ryu*.

THE ORIGIN of GOJU-RYU

Although his study of *Shuri-te* began during his childhood, as a young man, Master Higashionna also traveled to China where he took instruction in Chinese boxing. When he finally returned to Okinawa, he began combining the stronger elements of *tee* with what he had learned in China. The result was a new martial art form, informally called *Naha-te*, more suited to the needs of his country.

When, in 1929, delegates assembled in Kyoto for a national martial arts convention, Master Higashionna asked Master Chojun Miyagi, his most respected student, to represent him. Master Miyagi, however, was also unable to attend so he, in turn, appointed one of his pupils, Mr. Shinsato, as his replacement.

Martial artists from schools with impressive names flooded the convention. Mr. Shinsato, though, had no ready reply when asked the name of his style. Admitting his style had no formal name would damage the reputation of *Naha-te* and lower him to mere amateur status in the eyes of his fellow martial artists. Having no choice at all, then, Mr. Shinsato groped for an impromptu name and dubbed his style, *hanko-ryu* (half-hard style).

When Mr. Shinsato returned to Master Miyagi, he told him of the hastily chosen name. The master, finding it quite reasonable, quoted from the Chinese *Eight Poems of the Fists*: "Everything in the universe is breathing hard and soft . . . ," and so *Naha-te* formally took the name of *Goju-Ryu*.

Goju applies to society and karate alike. Only hardness or only softness creates an inability to deal effectively with the fluctuations of life. Courtesy is a small example of this. Its use can soften an otherwise hard transaction. In karate, too, hardness and softness combine in successful techniques. When preparing to block, the body is soft and inhaling. When attacking or punching, it becomes hard and exhaling. This existence of both hard and soft characterizes *Goju-Ryu* karate.

MASTER KANRYO HIGASHIONNA (1840—1910)

Master Kanryo Higashionna began his studies in the martial arts as a child. As a young man, however, he became a sailor on the *Shinko-Sen*, a vessel engaged in regular trading and cultural expeditions to China. On one of these expeditions, he bravely rescued a drowning child. When he returned the child to its parents, he discovered that Master Ryu, a renowned Chinese martial artist, was the boy's father. When a grateful Master Ryu offered Master Higashionna a reward, Master Higashionna asked for instruction in the art of Chinese boxing.

Master Higashionna trained under Master Ryu for thirty years. On his return to Okinawa, he began teaching the art of boxing. He decided, however, that although the boxing he had learned was excellent, it did not suit the needs of his native country. After much study and hard work, he succeeded in creating *Naha-te*, an improved art which combined the good points of karate with certain elements of Chinese boxing. For example, the form *Sanchin*, originally done with open hands, was changed to fists closed.

Master Higashionna's vision perceived a movement from technique to art, from individuals to groups. He implemented this improved and more practical art form into his teachings at the police and junior high schools. Thus began the realization of his vision. And, as his teachings spread farther and farther, so did his fame. Master Higashionna became known as a "Fist-Saint" and is recognized as the father of *Goju-Ryu*. Among his top students were Master Chojun Miyagi and Master Juhatsu Kyoda.

MASTER CHOJUN MIYAGI (1888–1953)

Independently wealthy, Chojun Miyagi was able to devote his life to the exclusive study of the martial arts. Unsurpassed as a teacher and developer of the art, he once said, "If I had devoted my time and wealth to some other enterprise, I would have been successful. But I devoted my life to mastering everything from Master Higashionna." And so he did. After his master's death, Master Miyagi journeyed to China twice to study and collect further literature on the martial arts. A pioneer in internationalizing karate, he also traveled to mainland Japan and Hawaii to spread its doctrine.

In 1933, when *Dai Nippon Butoku Kai* (the largest martial arts organization recognized by the pre-war Japanese government) was established, Master Miyagi, as the representative of the Okinawan martial artists, presented his article, " An Outline of Karate-Do."

As a result of his presentation, karate received formal recognition as a Japanese martial art. Master Miyagi himself was awarded the title, *Karate-Do Master*, the first master in the karate world so designated.

Although Master Miyagi's command of the art was profound, his greatest achievement was the organization of karate teaching methods. He introduced preparation exercises, supplementary exercises, *Hookiyu Kata* (unified kata), *kihon kata* (basic forms) and relaxing exercises, all truly epoch-making developments in karate teaching. In addition, his classes in junior high and police schools helped redefine karate's public image. At that time, public opinion held that karate would make a person poor or fond of quarreling. Master Miyagi's work, however, disproved these myths and presented a more accurate picture of karate as a martial art and physical exercise.

Although a master in the *Goju-Ryu* style (*Naha-te*), Master Chojun Miyagi wanted to study karate more completely. He visited the most respected master of *Shuri-te*, Master Anko Itosu, and asked for instruction. Master Itosu responded by saying, "You are a top disciple of Master Higashionna and you have mastered *Naha-te* techniques. You don't need to study with me. If you watch my techniques, you will see what I mean."

Master Miyagi persisted, however, and often visited Master Itosu to study *Shuri-te*. Master Itosu did not teach Master Miyagi physical techniques; rather, he taught the theory of techniques. Master Itosu's influence may be seen in Master Miyagi's *Hookiyu Kata* where the combination of hard and soft (as in *Gekisai* No. 1 and No. 2) reflect *Shuri-te's* movements.

While I was in my teens and twenties, Master Miyagi emphasized body building and practicing techniques, without theory. After my thirties, however, he said, "You have passed the period of training and from now on you should learn the theories and instructions." He then taught me new forms and instruction techniques better suited to modern times. After his 65th birthday, perhaps foreseeing the imminence of death, he talked for hours at our study sessions, sometimes from noon until midnight. During these intense discussions, I often forgot all other matters and became totally involved in our conversations.

When my face sometimes reflected boredom at Master Miyagi's repetition of certain things, he would say, "The same story heard during the twenties and then (again) during the thirties will seem different each time, both in understanding and impression. But, that is the secret. Also, any good theory is useless without actual application." From conversations such as these, I obtained an understanding of Master Miyagi's karate theories and I apply them now in practice. Had I mastered mere technique without theory, I would have ended up merely a simple recorder, mechanically teaching what I had learned without the creative development of ideas.

HOOKIYU KATA
unified kata

NECESSITY of UNIFIED KATA and its MEANING

Devising a system of kata suitable for students of all schools is a monumental task involving a wide range of styles. Still, to maintain a set of universal standards to grade any one's ability, it becomes necessary to establish a unified kata that takes all styles into account.

Lacking any systematic program for teaching, karate masters have sometimes taught difficult classical kata to beginners ill-prepared to handle such instruction. A unified kata is necessary to give beginners a solid foundation on which they may later build more complex forms. Beginners should learn unified kata first. After this, they may pursue either the martial arts aspect of karate (in which they may study classic styles in depth) or the sports aspect or both.

Many students also attempt free-fighting and sparring, having mastered only the sequence of kata. They do not understand the real meaning of technique but mistakenly feel themselves adequately prepared for fighting. Thus, they become sloppy, caring more for free-fighting than good karate. Unified kata is necessary, therefore, to maintain the theory and technique of karate.

The unified kata and kumite (pre-arranged sparring) presented herein have been well-received by students for the last twenty years. Although these kata should be sanctioned by all major karate leaders, the karate community is not yet ready for such a move. The primary goals at this time, however, do not include immediate approval from karate masters. Instead, popularization of traditional karate, improvement of physical health and promotion of world-wide friendship and understanding are the larger goals of this text.

MERITS of UNIFIED KATA

The system of *Hookiyu Kata* is preferable to those currently enjoying popularity for the following reasons:

1. Most methods of karate instruction today emphasize either classic kata or free-fighting competition, both designed for the advanced student. As many women and children study karate, these methods inadequately provide for differences in prior experience and physical capability. Using Unified Kata, however, which emphasizes a system of basic calisthenics, everyone—regardless of physical condition—can practice and enjoy karate.

2. As this curriculum of Unified Kata is systematic, one can easily and progressively move from basic to advanced stages. Using Unified Kata, one can also work alone perfecting techniques.

3. As a compulsory part of primary karate instruction, Unified Kata becomes the basis of all karate techniques, including classic kata and sparring competition. Under this curriculum, fairer ranking promotions become a more realistic possibility. With all performers taught and judged by the same set of standards, the inherent discrepancies and prejudices arising from comparision of different styles are eliminated.

4. Unified Kata paves the road toward future entry in the Olympic games. Turning this into a viable concern, however, depends on a uniform system of instruction and standard criteria for judging performances.

5. As music, physical training and the martial arts are inter-related, this curriculum facilitates setting certain kata to music, an enjoyable exercise for both performer and audience alike. A *rhythm karate*, devised by Mr. Seihin Yamauchi and this author has proved beneficial to physical development and artistic accomplishment.

THE CURRICULUM and its COMBINATION

Hookiya Kata, related to many styles because it adopts techniques from classic kata, is set up progressively. Students necessarily begin with basic techniques and move to advanced sets from there. This system of gradual advancement has proved successful in providing the serious student with a thorough, solid knowledge of the techniques of karate.

Instead of just numerical designations, the kata have been given different names (such as Gekisai, Gekiha or Kakuha) to avoid confusion. Master Chojun Miyagi devised Kata No. 3 and No. 4 which he called Gekisai No. 1 and Gekisai No. 2. For easier kata, I created Hookiyu Kata No. 1 and No. 2. To add more difficult ones, I set up Kata No. 5 through No. 9. The curriculum combinations should be arranged as follows: Hookiyu Kata No. 1,

Grade	Kaishu Kata	Kiso Kumite	Bunkai Kumite
1	No. 1 (Hookiyu Kata No. 1)	No. 1	No. 1
2	No. 2 (Hookiyu Kata No. 2)	No. 2	No. 2
3	No. 3 (Gekisai No. 1)	No. 3	No. 3
4	No. 4 (Gekisai No. 2)	No. 4	No. 4
5	No. 5 (Gekisai No. 3)	No. 5	No. 5
6	No. 6 (Gekiha No. 1)	No. 6	No. 6
7	No. 7 (Gekiha No. 2)	No. 7	No. 7
8	No. 8 (Kakuha No. 1)	No. 8	No. 8
9	No. 9 (Kakuha No. 2)	No. 9	No. 9

Kiso Kumite No. 1 and Bunkai Kumite No. 1 taught at the first grade; Hookiyu Kata No. 2, Kiso Kumite No. 2 and Bunkai Kumite No. 2 taught at the second; Gekisai No. 1, Kiso Kumite No. 3 and Bunkai Kumite No. 3 taught at the third and so forth. The phases of training are set up progressively according to difficulty of execution.

Before the development of this curriculum, only kata was taught. The Bunkai Kumite was added later to illuminate more clearly the meaning of the Kata. When it seemed that Bunkai

Kumite was a trifle difficult for beginners, Kiso Kumite was also added.

Please note that because Hookiyu Kata No. 1 and Hookiyu Kata No. 2 are very similarly executed, the latter has not been included in this text. Instead, Gekisai No. 1 and its Bunkai (from grade three) have been presented. The corresponding grade three Kiso Kumite No. 3, however, will be discussed at a later date and the student is asked to master Kiso Kumite No. 2 (included herein and from grade two) first.

RANKING SYSTEM and CURRICULUM

Promotion in the ranking system is based on the student's curricular proficiency. He will advance in rank according to his progressive mastery of grades one through nine. The corresponding ranks and grades are as follows:

Grade One — 9th Kyu test subjects

Grade Two — 8th Kyu test subjects

Grade Three — 7th Kyu test subjects

Grade Four — 6th Kyu test subjects

Grade Five — 5th Kyu test subjects

Grade Six — 4th Kyu test subjects

Grade Seven — 3rd Kyu test subjects

Grade Eight — 2nd Kyu test subjects

Grade Nine — 1st Kyu test subjects

Grade Ten — First degree black belt subjects

The student who has mastered the techniques and kata of grade one will be promoted to ninth Kyu; one who has mastered grade two will be promoted to eighth Kyu and so on. When the student completes grade nine, he becomes a first Kyu and is eligible for a black belt at his next promotion.

HOOKIYU KATA SUBJECTS

The subjects and their order of instruction are: (1) warming-up exercise; (2) supplementary exercise; (3) main exercise and (4) relaxing exercise.

The warming-up exercise prepares the student for the main exercise by enabling him to stretch his muscles and soften his joints. It also stimulates metabolism and circulation.

The supplementary exercises, derived apart from main exercise kata, may be done alone or in *kumite* (two-man tandem) and involve the use of weapons such as *makiwara, chishi, sashi,* etc.

The main exercise consists of either classic kata or *hookiyu kata.* The primary concern herein is hookiyu kata, which may be broken down into *kaishu kata* and *kumite kata* as follows:

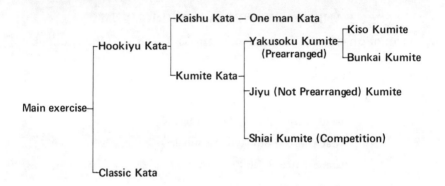

Kaishu kata, prearranged sets of combative movements performed by one person, consist of basic punches, blocks, *shuto-uchis* (chop strikes) and kicks. Totaling nine in all, kaishu kata are performed in four directions: right, left, forward and backward.

Kumite, which involves two men, may be broken down into three categories: (1) prearranged or *yakusoku* kumite; (2) spontaneous or *jiyu kumite;* and (3) competition or *shiai kumite.* Prearranged kumite, in turn, may be classified as either *kiso kumite* or *bunkai kumite.*

The techniques of kiso kumite simply combine and incorporate, in tandem, the beginning movements of kaishu kata. There are a total of nine kiso kumite also.

Bunkai kumite, prearranged sets of techniques which follow the kata, enable students to practice timing, focus on techniques in a more realistic situation and learn the purpose of each movement. There are nine bunkai kumite exercises.

Kaishu kata, kiso kumite and bunkai kumite are practiced together and, in this curriculum, are set in stages.

Relaxing exercises, performed after the main exercise, are those specialized calisthenics which loosen up joints and muscles, allowing the body to cool off gradually and release tension.

BASICS

Posture

Good posture, basic to all movements, helps maintain balance. Loss of balance is one of the causes of defeat, and learning to maintain equilibrium through good posture helps win competitions.

Bad posture is easy to fall into. As a result, observe the following:

Try to keep your chin pulled in. Do not bend your neck or stick your chin out.

Keep your chest open wide. Do not let it cave in.

Pull your hips up and thrust your pelvis forward. Do not let your buttocks protrude backward.

Focus on an object at eye level. Try not to look down.

Power and Breathing

Without power, karate loses effectiveness; without speed, the student is sorely disadvantaged. The unity of balance between power and speed increases the effect of karate. This unity and balance, however, cannot be attained without correct, natural breathing. It is, therefore, necessary to practice breathing naturally.

Certainty, Power and Speed

Power may be cultivated through exercise, training with equipment and correct natural breathing. Initially, practice your techniques correctly but without power. Then, gradually add both power and speed. As you progress, slowly trim off any unnecessary power, add more speed and practice your timing of both. This sort of training proves effective preparation for actual sparring.

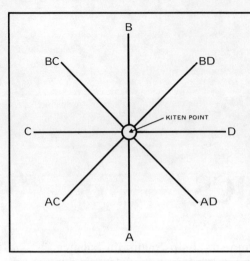

ENBUSEN DIAGRAM

This diagram shows *enbusen lines* or the directions of kata. Kata, performed in these directions only, begin at the center circle which is called the *kiten point*. Stand here facing in the direction of enbusen line A (forward in the photographs). This position determines all others: to the student's back is B; to his right, C; to his left, D; and so forth.

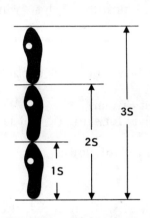

FOOT SCALE

Your foot length or *sokucho* determines stance measurements. One sokucho (1 S) is one foot length, two sokuchos (2 S) are two foot lengths. The spot on the footmark indicates the ball of the foot (BF).

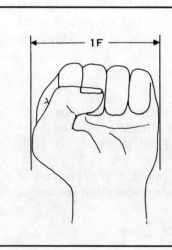

FIST SCALE

As with the foot, the student's fist also fixes measurement. The outermost perimeters of the student's clenched fist, from one edge to the other, determine fist length (see diagram). One fist (1 F) is one fist length; two fists (2 F) are two fist lengths.

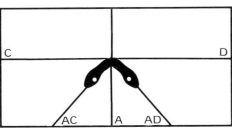

MUSUBIDACHI STANCE

Place your heels together on the kiten point, with the balls of your feet (BF) on enbusen lines AC and AD as indicated.

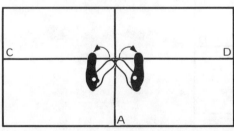

HEIKODACHI STANCE

From the musubidachi stance, pivot on the balls of your feet, moving your heels outward to parallel positions. Do not raise your heels but slide them on the floor when pivoting.

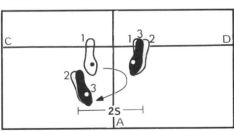

KIHONDACHI STANCE

From the (1) heikodachi stance, (2) step forward with your right foot, pointing your toes inward. As you step forward, bring your right foot as close as possible to your left foot and bring it out again in a semi-circular manner. Slide your foot across the floor. Do not lift it up. Make sure the heel of your right foot and the toe of your left end on a line parallel to enbusen line CD. Now, (3) turn your heels inward while bringing your hips upward. The distance between the outside perimeters of your feet should be 2.0 S. Keep your heels within this 2.0 S perimeter and the weight of your body centered. Do not lean forward or backward.

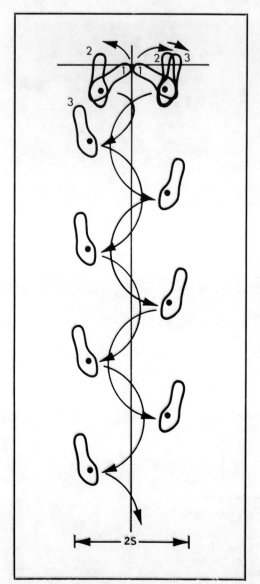

BASIC WALKING

The (1) musubidachi, (2) heikodachi, (3) kihondachi preparatory sequence is indicated in the diagram. Basic walking really begins, then, with the kihondachi stance. From position No. 3 (where the right foot is forward), bring your left foot forward to a second kihondachi stance. Repetition of the kihondachi stance, alternating right foot and left foot, produces basic walking. Although the second movements of kihondachi are not shown in the diagram, do not forget to turn the heels inward at each step while bringing the hip up. As you walk, keep your eyes focused straight ahead and your weight centered. To walk backwards, reverse the movements, bringing your feet inward and back in a sliding semi-circular motion. NOTE: Bend your knees slightly but do not tense them.

SIDE VIEW

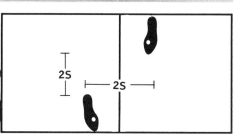

ZENKUTSU DACHI STANCE

Both the distance between the heel of your forward foot and the toes of your rear foot and the distance between the outside edges of each foot should be 2.0 S. Point your toes inward and your heels outward as shown and bend your front knee over the big toe of your forward foot. Do not bend your rear knee.

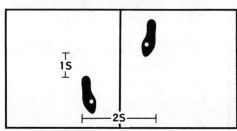

SHO (SMALL) ZENKUTSU DACHI STANCE

The movements here follow those of the zenkutsu dachi stance, only the distance between the heel of the forward foot and the toes of the rear foot should be 1.0 S, not 2.0 S. The distance between the outside edges of both feet, however, remains 2.0 S.

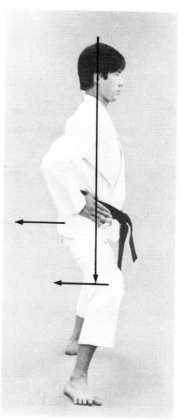

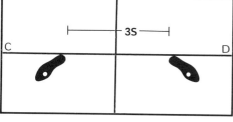

SHIKODACHI STANCE

Place your feet, toes outward, at forty-five degree angles to enbusen lines C and D (see diagram). Your heels should be 3.0 S apart. With your lower legs perpendicular to the floor, form an angle of forty-five degrees with your thighs and the floor. Push your buttocks backward, keeping your spine straight and lower back tight. Pull your knees backward.

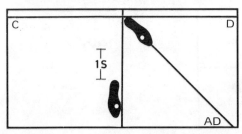

RENOJI DACHI STANCE

Place your forward foot along enbusen line A and your rear foot along enbusen line AD (or AC, depending on whether you assume the right or left foot forward position). The distance between the heel of your forward foot and the toes of your rear foot should be 1.0 S. Keep your rear knee straight and bend your forward knee over the big toe of the forward foot.

HACHIJI DACHI STANCE

Set your feet, toes outward, at forty-five degree angles to enbusen lines C and D (or parallel to lines AC and AD), with heels 1.5 S apart.

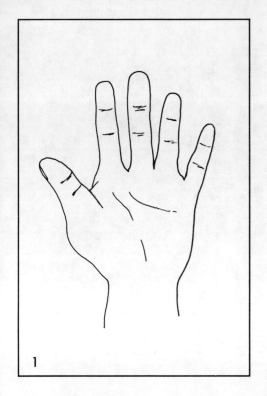

1

HOW TO MAKE THE
SEIKEN FIST

(1) Open your hand, extending your fingers. (2-3) Beginning with the little finger, tightly roll each digit toward your palm. Try to tuck your

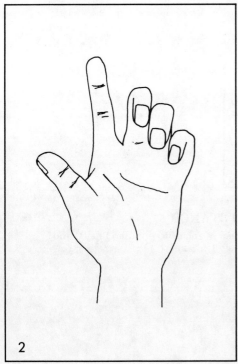

2

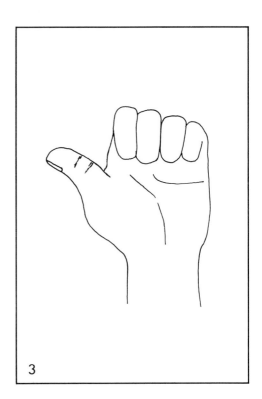

3

nails into your hand so that they cannot be seen. (4) Close your thumb over the first two fingers. Do not let your thumb stick out.

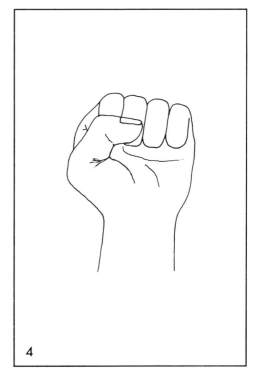

4

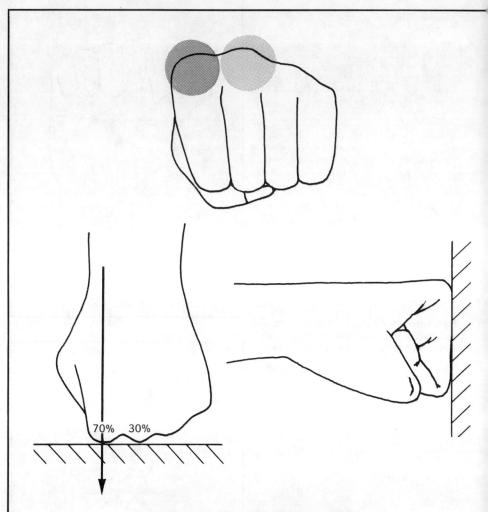

70%   30%

HOW TO USE THE SEIKEN FIST

Do not bend your wrist. In striking, do not use your knuckles or finger joints alone but make contact with the entire area of your first two fingers, as shown. Primary contact, however, should come from your first two knuckles —see diagram. Seventy percent (70%) of the power comes from the impact of the first knuckle. Thirty percent (30%) comes from the second knuckle. In the kata and kumite that follow, the student will execute punches, blocks and all clenched fist positions with the SEIKEN fist.

KAMAE OR BASIC
ON-GUARD POSITION

Use your hands to make seiken fists. Assume the kihondachi stance with your right foot forward. RIGHT HAND: Bending your elbow ninety degrees, push it forward a distance of 1.0 F from your torso. Your fist, palm toward the ceiling, should be directly in front of your right shoulder. An imaginary line drawn from the edge of your right shoulder to the little finger of your right hand should be perpendicular to your body. LEFT HAND: Pull your left fist, palm toward the ceiling, near your left armpit. Keep your elbow down and to the back. Turn your fist counterclockwise to a slight angle. It should not protrude from the chest line. Keep your shoulders level. Do not raise them.

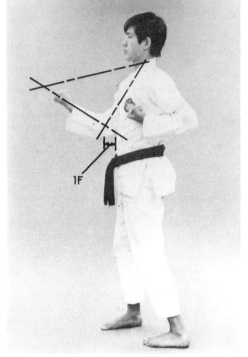

BEGINNING AND ENDING FORMALITIES

The kata and bunkai presented herein are preceded by the beginning formality and followed by the ending formality. The BEGINNING FORMALITY usually consists of the following sequence: From the initial position of attention, the student bows and returns to the position of attention. Then, he assumes the ready stance, moves into the opening position and takes up the kamae or on-guard stance. The movements of the ENDING FORMALITY are those of the beginning formality executed in reverse order. After completing his kata, bunkai or kumite, the student either assumes the kamae or on-guard stance or moves directly into the closing position. Then, he takes up the ready stance and ends the formality with the attention-bowing-attention sequence.

BEGINNING FORMALITY

(1) Assume the position of ATTENTION by placing your feet in the musubidachi stance and extending your arms along the sides of your body, hands open, palms to the inside. (2) BOW by bending forward at the waist 15 to 20 degrees. Keep your eyes focused straight ahead. (3) Straighten up and return to the position of ATTENTION. (4) Enter the READY position by bringing both hands, palms toward you, over your groin. Place your left hand over your right so that the middle knuckle of your left hand falls directly over the middle knuckle of your right. The distance between your hands and your body should be 1.5 to 2.0 F. (5) To OPEN, pivot counterclockwise on your right foot and clockwise on your left into a heikodachi stance. As you do so, extend both arms so that your clenched fists, palms toward you, are 1.5 to 2.0 F away from your upper thighs and slightly to the outside. (6) Pivot slightly on one foot and step forward with the other to assume the KAMAE or ON-GUARD position. Bring your arms up accordingly, one leading slightly, one withdrawn.

1

4

40

2

3

5

6

1

ENDING FORMALITY

(1) From the last technique of the exercise, assume the KAMAE OR ON-GUARD POSITION. (2) Or, you may move directly from the last technique of the kata, kumite or bunkai into the CLOSING position. Sweep your open hands out toward your sides and upward in a semi-circular motion to a point in front of your chest. Palms toward you, place your left hand under your right so that the middle knuckle of your left

2

3

hand is directly under the middle knuckle of your right. The elbow of each arm should form a ninety-degree angle and the distance between each elbow and your torso should be 1.0 F. (3) Bring your hands down, still right over left as in the closing, over your groin into the READY stance. (4) Complete the formality by bringing your hands to your side to execute the (a) ATTEN-TION, (b) BOWING, (c) ATTEN-TION sequence.

4

SIDE VIEW

PUNCHES

The basic punching movements, CHUDAN TSUKI (middle or chest punch), JODAN TSUKI (high or head punch) and GEDAN TSUKI (low or stomach punch) are very similar. They differ only in target level: in chudan tsuki, the punching arm is thrown out on a level even with the center of your solar plexus; in jodan tsuki, even with your mouth and in gedan tsuki, even with your navel. In all cases, while one arm executes the punch, the other simultaneously withdraws (with the fist pulled toward the armpit, elbow down and to the back).

CHUDAN TSUKI
(MIDDLE PUNCH)

In a left chudan tsuki, extend your right fist as shown, palm toward the floor, elbow straight. Pull your left fist, palm up and turned outward, back toward your left armpit, keeping your elbow down and to the back. Do not raise your shoulders and keep your wrists straight. To execute the punch with your left hand, simultaneously and with an equal amount of speed, pull your right hand back toward your right armpit while throwing your left out on a level even with your solar plexus (the center of your body). As both hands move, twist the fist of each over clockwise. Again, do not move your shoulders. At the end of the punch, your left arm should be fully extended; your left fist,

FRONT VIEW

SIDE VIEW

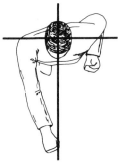

palm toward the floor, should be on a plane even with your solar plexus. Your right fist, palm toward the ceiling and outward, should be pulled back toward your right armpit. Keep your right elbow down and to the back.

To punch with your right hand, simply repeat the above, reversing the movements of your right and left hands. However, while you simultaneously throw your right fist out and pull your left fist back, turn your hands counterclockwise instead of clockwise.

At first, practice punching slowly. Concentrate on executing the movements correctly. Add power and speed gradually. Do not strike objects until you acquire proper timing of power and speed.

JODAN TSUKI
(HIGH PUNCH)

The technique here is the same as that used in chudan tsuki. However, instead of throwing the punching arm out on a level even with your solar plexus, throw it out on a level even with your mouth.

SIDE VIEW

GEDAN TSUKI
(LOW PUNCH)

The technique here is the same as that of chudan tsuki and jodan tsuki, however, your punching arm is thrown out on a level even with your navel.

BLOCKS

The movements of CHUDAN UKE (middle or chest block), JODAN UKE (high or head block) and GEDAN UKE (low or stomach block) are basically the same. In all three, both arms cross over the front of the chest, one arm covering the center of the body, the other moving into the block. They differ only in the ultimate level of the blocking arm—high, middle, low.

CHUDAN UKE (MIDDLE BLOCK)

To block to the middle left, (1) begin in the kamae or on-guard position, right

hand forward. (2) Bring your right fist, palm toward you, down across your chest, passing the point just below your wrist over your solar plexus. Simultaneously, bring your left hand up, crossing it over your right. (3) Bring your right elbow down and to the back and your right fist, palm upward, back toward your right armpit. Twist your left forearm outward and your left elbow inward to block. Remember to keep your wrist straight. In its completed form, the chudan block is similar to the kamae or on-guard position.

To block to the middle right, (4—6) repeat the above, reversing right and left.

1

2

3

SIDE VIEWS

JODAN UKE
(HIGH BLOCK)

To execute a high left block, (1—2) begin by moving your hands as in the chudan uke. (3) However, as your left hand passes over your right, follow a line along the center of your body and thrust it up to forehead level. Simultaneously, twist it clockwise so that your palm initially turned toward you, faces upward and away from you. Position your right hand as in the chudan

4   5   6

1.5 F

uke. (4) Complete the block by aligning the point just below your left wrist with the middle of your body. Hold it forty-five degrees above and 1.5 F away from your head. Again, remember to keep your wrists straight.

To block to the high right, (5—6) repeat the above, reversing right and left. Twist your right wrist counterclockwise as it moves upward.

SIDE VIEWS

GEDAN UKE
(LOW BLOCK)

To execute a block to the low left, (1) begin in the kamae stance, right hand forward. (2-3) Without moving your right hand, raise your left hand so that the point just below your wrist is aligned with the center of your forehead, palm toward you. Now, (4) bring your right fist down across your chest and back toward your right armpit (as in chudan uke and jodan uke). At the same time, bring your left fist down over your right, turning your left forearm

downward and outward to block. Complete the movement by (5) extending your left (or blocking) arm. At the end of the block, the distance between your left wrist and outer left thigh should be 1.5—2.0 F with your arms forming a forty-five degree angle with your body. Synchronize the movements of your left and right arms so that both reach the position of completion simultaneously.   CONTINUED

SIDE VIEWS CONT.

CONTINUED

To execute a low block to the right, again, repeat the above, reversing your left and right hands. From the kamae stance, left hand forward, (6) raise your right hand up toward your head, palm toward you. (7-8) Bring your left fist down across your chest and back toward your left armpit while simultaneously bringing your right fist down over your left. (9) Complete the block by turning your right forearm outward and extending your fist downward near your thigh.

The following sections include the elementary and intermediate levels of Shorei-Kan Karate and use Hookiyu Kata as their point of departure. The text is written in a step by step manner, designed to facilitate a clear understanding on the student's part and promote enjoyment of karate either alone or with others, any time or any place. It must be read in sequence so that new techniques explained prior to their entry in subject discussions will be understood fully before execution. Kata should be practiced many times before you study bunkai kumite. Do not attempt covering too many subjects too soon. Practice slowly, step by step.

HOOKIYU KATA NO. 1 AND ITS BUNKAI

At the first grade or level, the beginner studies Hookiyu Kata No. 1. In it, he learns to use the basics in a series of movements while maintaining good posture and proper breathing. He also learns to develop the speed, power and timing essential to proper execution of his techniques.

Then, having mastered the kata, he studies the corresponding bunkai (Bunkai Kumite No. 1) and applies his knowledge to the two-man tandem exercise.

1

NEW TECHNIQUES INTRODUCED

Other than the basic blocks and punches, two techniques are introduced in Hookiyu Kata No. 1 — SUIHEI SHUTO UCHI (side chop) and MOROTE TSUKI (double punch).

MOROTE TSUKI
(DOUBLE PUNCH)

(1) While in the "ready" position of morote tsuki, the elbows of both your arms are pulled back and down, with your fists up against either side of your chest and even with your solar plexus. Both arms should touch your body. The palm of your right hand should face the ceiling while the palm of your left hand should face the floor. The upward/downward positions of your fists may be reversed. Simply remember that the hand that has its palm facing the

SIDE VIEW

floor delivers the upper punch while the hand that has its palm facing the ceiling delivers the lower punch. In this case, the left hand will deliver the upper punch while the right hand simultaneously delivers the lower punch. (2) Aim the upper punch to your opponent's heart level and the lower punch to his belt or appendix level. Do not fully extend either elbow. Remember to keep the shoulder delivering the upper punch down —do not raise it. Also, keep your wrists straight.

SIDE VIEW

SUIHEI SHUTO UCHI
(SIDE CHOP)

To apply a suihei shuto uchi with your right hand, assume the kamae position, right hand forward. (1) Bring your right hand, palm open and facing the ceiling, to your left shoulder. Do not place your hand against your shoulder but hold it loosely in front of you at that level. Keep your wrists straight. Your eyes and head should be turned to the right, toward the target. (2) Now, sweep your right arm out, opening your chest wide. As you sweep outward, twist your hand and forearm so that the palm of your hand faces downward. The outer edge of your hand executes the blow. Extend your arm as you complete the chop but do not raise your shoulders.

A left shuto uchi is executed in exactly the same manner, using your left hand instead of your right.

HOW TO READ THE DIAGRAMS

Kata are shown on the upper level. The corresponding movements of the bunkai kumite, the kata exercise done in two-man tandem, are presented immediately below to help the student see more clearly the relationship of one to the other. However, although the kata and bunkai have been presented in parallel sequence, bunkai should not be practiced until performance of the kata has been mastered.

In the bunkai (and all two-man sequences throughout the book), separate footwork diagrams and hand movements have been included for "A", the figure shown on the left, and "B", the figure shown on the right.

The symbols presented with the footwork diagrams indicate the following:

● technique executed in place

⟷ technique executed following a step in the direction of the arrow(s)

⊙ technique executed following a pivot

For example, 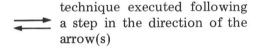 means that A and B move toward each other. A.B→ means that both A and B move in the same direction: that is, A steps forward while B steps backward. Also, unless otherwise indicated, all steps are taken in the manner described in the section on basic walking.

In addition, the basic punches and blocks, as used in the kata, bunkai and kumite, do not always begin in the starting positions described earlier. The general technique, however, is basic enough to make the details of moving from one position to another self-evident. As a result, explication of handwork will be given only where deemed necessary.

KATA NOS. 1–3

Execute the beginning formality sequence of (1) attention, (2) bowing, and (3) a return to attention. The footwork diagrams should be self-explanatory as they are, very simply, continuous sequential placements of positions previously discussed.

BUNKAI NOS. 1–3

Both **A** and **B**: Execute the beginning formality sequence of (1) attention, (2) bowing, and (3) a return to attention.

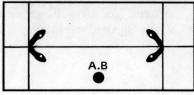

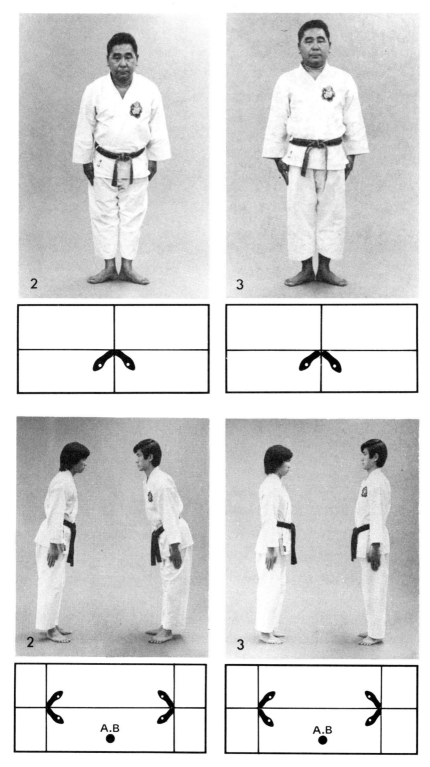

KATA NOS. 4–6

Complete the beginning formality sequence of (4) ready, (5) opening, and finally, (6) kamae or on-guard, right foot forward.

BUNKAI NOS. 4–6

Both **A** and **B**: Complete the beginning formality sequence of (4) ready, (5) opening, and finally, (6) kamae or on-guard, right foot forward.

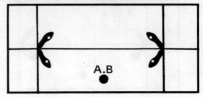

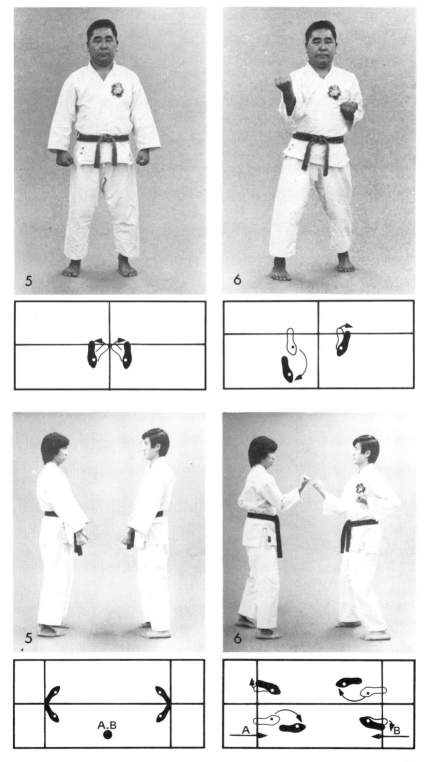

63

KATA NO. 7

From a right kamae or on-guard position, slide your right foot .5 S on a line parallel to enbusen line AD. Now, pivot counterclockwise on both feet into a kihondachi stance in the direction of enbusen line D. From a kihondachi stance with your right foot forward, you will have moved into a kihondachi stance with your left foot forward. Please note, however, that in this instance, assuming the second kihondachi stance does not involve sliding your foot forward in a semi-circular motion. On completing the pivot, pull your right fist back and execute a jodan (high) block with your left.

KATA NO. 8

Step forward with your right foot. As you step, execute a right chudan (middle) punch.

KATA NO. 9

Swing your right foot back and to the right (in the direction of enbusen line C). As you do so, pivot clockwise on your left foot into a shikodachi stance, placing both heels along enbusen line CD. Then, execute a left gedan (low) block. Keep your eyes and head turned to your left (in the direction of enbusen line D and toward the imaginary on-coming gedan punch).

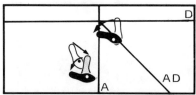

BUNKAI NO. 7

Both **A** and **B** begin facing each other in the right kihondachi stance. **B:** Move toward **A**, stepping forward with your left foot into a left kihondachi stance. Execute a left jodan (high) punch. **A:** From the right kihondachi stance, step backward with your right foot and block to the high left (jodan block).

BUNKAI NO. 8

A: Step forward with your right foot and throw a right chudan (middle) punch. **B:** In response to **A**'s movement, step backward with your left foot and put up a right chudan (middle) block.

BUNKAI NO. 9

B: From the kihondachi stance, pivot clockwise on your right foot stepping forward forty-five degrees with your left into a shikodachi position. Hit toward **A** with a left gedan (low) punch. **A:** From your kihondachi stance, pivot counterclockwise on your left foot, stepping back with your right foot forty-five degrees into a shikodachi position. As you step back, block to the low left (gedan block).

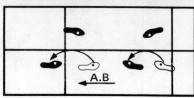

KATA NO. 10
Move out of the shikodachi stance by pivoting clockwise on the ball of your right foot. Bring your left foot toward it into a right kihondachi stance in the direction of enbusen line C. At the same time, execute a right jodan (high) block.

KATA NO. 11
Step forward with your left foot in the direction of enbusen line C, throwing a chudan (middle) punch with your left hand.

KATA NO. 12
Swing your left foot back and to your left (to enbusen line D). As you do so, pivot counterclockwise on your right foot, moving into a shikodachi stance with both heels along enbusen line CD. As your feet move into the shikodachi stance, block to the low right (gedan block), keeping your head and eyes to the right (in the direction of enbusen line C or toward the imaginary on-coming blow).

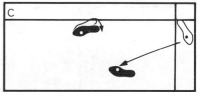

BUNKAI NO. 10
A: Pivot clockwise slightly on your left foot. Step forward with your right, moving out of the shikodachi position back into your original right kihondachi stance. As you do so, execute a right jodan (high) punch. B: Pivot counterclockwise on your right and step backward with your left foot, moving out of the shikodachi position back into your original right kihondachi stance. Counter A's right jodan punch with a right jodan (high) block.

BUNKAI NO. 11
B: Step forward with your left foot and throw out a left chudan (middle) punch. A: Step back with your right foot and put up a left chudan (middle) block.

BUNKAI NO. 12
A: Pivot counterclockwise on your left foot, stepping forward with your right forty-five degrees into a second shikodachi stance. Put down a right gedan (low) punch. B: Pivot clockwise slightly on your right foot, and step backward on your left forty-five degrees into a second shikodachi stance. Block A's right gedan punch with a right gedan (low) block.

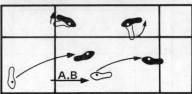

66

KATA NO. 13

From the shikodachi position, pivot counter-clockwise on your right foot, stepping with your left into a left kihondachi in the direction of enbusen line A. As your feet move, throw up a left chudan (middle) block. NOTE: As you step with your left foot, do not forget to slide it forward past your right in a semi-circular movement.

KATA NO. 14

Remain in the left kihondachi position and put down a left gedan (low) block.

KATA NO. 15

Still in the left kihondachi position, execute a right gedan (low) punch.

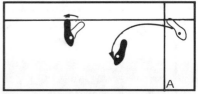

BUNKAI NO. 13

B: Return to the left kihondachi stance. Pivot counterclockwise slightly on your right foot and step forward with your left. Complete a left chudan (middle) punch. A: Return to the left kihondachi stance also by pivoting clockwise on your left foot and stepping back on your right. Counter B's left chudan punch with a left chudan (middle) block.

BUNKAI NO. 14

B: Move out of the left chudan punch and perform a right gedan (low) punch. Keep your feet in the kihondachi position. A: Remain in the left kihondachi stance and move your arms into a left gedan (low) block.

BUNKAI NO. 15

A: Without moving your feet, execute a right gedan (low) punch. B: Step in place also and throw out a left gedan (low) block to stop A's blow.

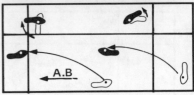

69

KATA NO. 16

Pivot clockwise on your left foot until it forms a forty-five degree angle with enbusen line CD. Simultaneously, sweep your right foot up toward your left knee, the edge of your right foot parallel to the floor, the bottom of your right foot facing your left knee. The trunk of your body should now face in the direction of enbusen line C. As your feet move, keep your left hand back and bring your open right hand, palm toward the ceiling, to your left shoulder to prepare for a right shuto uchi (side chop). Turn your head in the direction of enbusen line B.

KATA NO. 17

Stamp your right foot down into a soto hachiji dachi position, the heel of your right foot against enbusen line CD. The heels of both feet should now lie on a line parallel to enbusen line AB. Simultaneously, execute a neck level right shuto uchi (side chop). Pull your left hand farther back as the blow is delivered. Open your chest wide.

KATA NO. 18

Pivot clockwise slightly on your right foot and move your left into a left kihondachi stance in the direction of enbusen line B. You should now be turned around and facing what was initially behind you. As you pivot, withdraw your right hand and slowly move into a left chudan (middle) block.

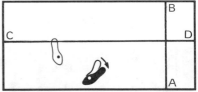

BUNKAI NO. 16

A: Pivot clockwise on your right foot, sweep up your left and assume the shuto uchi (side chop) ready position. **B:** Pivot clockwise on both feet into a sho zenkutsu dachi stance and prepare yourself for the execution of a left jodan (high) block.

BUNKAI NO. 17

A: Stamp your left foot down into a soto hachiji dachi position and chop. **B:** Maintain your sho zenkutsu dachi stance and stop **A**'s shuto uchi with the left jodan block.

BUNKAI NO. 18

A: Pivot clockwise slightly on your left foot, moving your right forward into a right kihondachi stance. Strike toward **B** with a right chudan (middle) punch. **B:** Block **A**'s right chudan punch with a right chudan (middle) block. As you protect yourself, step back on your left foot, pivoting counterclockwise with your right into a right kihondachi position.

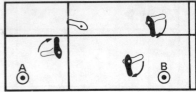

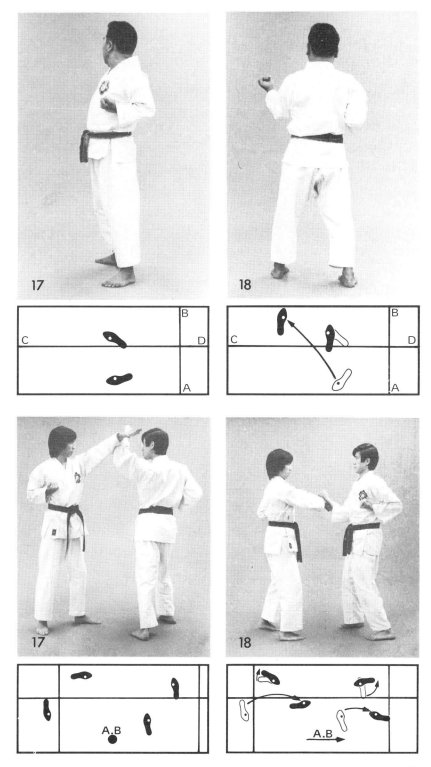

KATA NO. 19
While remaining in the left kihondachi stance, move your left arm out of the chudan (middle) block into a left gedan (low) block.

KATA NO. 20
Continue to maintain the left kihondachi stance. Execute a right gedan (low) punch while pulling your left fist up toward your armpit, elbow down and to the back.

KATA NO. 21
Pivot slightly on the ball of your left foot, moving your left heel clockwise in the direction of enbusen line BC until your foot again approximates a forty-five degree angle with enbusen line CD. Simultaneously, sweep your right foot up toward your left knee so the edge of your right foot is roughly parallel to the floor and the bottom of your right foot faces your left knee. At this point, the trunk of your body should face in the direction of enbusen line D. As your feet move, keep your left hand in position. Bring your open right hand, palm toward the ceiling, to your left shoulder to prepare for a right shuto uchi (side chop). Turn your head to what is now your right (in the direction of enbusen line A).

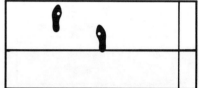

BUNKAI NO. 19
A: Keeping your feet in the right kihondachi stance, move out of the right chudan punch into a left gedan (low) punch. B: Maintain your right kihondachi also and put down a right gedan (low) block.

BUNKAI NO. 20
B: Execute a left gedan (low) punch. Your feet remain in the right kihondachi stance. A: Follow your left gedan punch with a right gedan (low) block. Your feet also remain in the right kihondachi stance.

BUNKAI NO. 21
B: Pivoting counterclockwise on your left foot, sweep your right foot up and prepare yourself for the execution of a right-handed shuto uchi (side chop). A: Pivot counterclockwise on the balls of both feet into a left sho zenkutsu dachi stance. Assume the "ready" position for a right jodan (high) block.

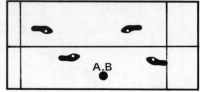

20

21

20

21

A.B

A

B

BC

B

C

D

A

KATA NO. 22

Stamp your right foot down into a soto hachi-ji dachi position with the heel of your right foot against enbusen line CD. The heels of both feet should lie on a line parallel to enbusen line AB. While you stamp, execute a neck level shuto uchi (side chop) with your right hand. Pull your left fist and elbow, farther back as the blow is delivered and open your chest wide.

KATA NO. 23

Move into a zenkutsu dachi position by pivoting clockwise on your left foot. As you do so, bring your right foot sharply around and behind you about 2.0 S in the direction of enbusen line B. You should be facing in the direction of enbusen line A once again. Now, execute a left chudan (middle) block.

KATA NO. 24

While maintaining the zenkutsu dachi stance, move out of the completed chudan block into the morote tsuki (double punch) "ready" position. Bring your left fist, palm toward the ceiling, back toward your left armpit, elbow down and to the rear. At the same time, twist your right fist so its palm faces the floor and pull it toward your right armpit. Pull your right elbow down and to the rear also.

BUNKAI NO. 22

B: Stamp your right foot down into a soto hachiji dachi position and complete the shuto uchi (side chop) with your right hand. A: Execute the jodan (high) block to counter B's shuto uchi.

BUNKAI NO. 23

A: Move into a left kihondachi by pivoting clockwise on your right foot and stepping toward B with your left (you should now face him directly). As your feet move, strike toward B with a left chudan (middle) punch. B: Stop A's left chudan punch with a left chudan (middle) block. As you do so, step out of the soto hachiji dachi stance by pivoting clockwise slightly on your left foot. Step back with your right forty-five degrees into a left zenkutsu dachi stance.

BUNKAI NO. 24

B: Pull both hands toward you in preparation for a morote tsuki (double punch) with your right hand intended for A's heart and your left intended for his stomach or belt level. A: Maintain the left kihondachi stance, keeping your left arm extended as at the completion of the left chudan punch.

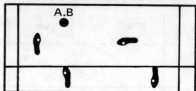

KATA NO. 25

Execute the morote tsuki (double punch), delivering your right hand out at heart level and undercutting your left hand, with elbow bent, at appendix level.

KATA NO. 26

While still in the zenkutsu dachi stance, begin the movements of the ending formality. Sweep both arms out to your sides and bring them up to a level even with your chest. Place your open right hand over your left as discussed in the section on closing hands. Remember that your elbows should be bent at ninety-degree angles.

KATA NO. 27

From the zenkutsu dachi stance, assume the musubidachi position. Pivot counterclockwise on the ball of your left foot as you bring your right foot forward. As the heels of both feet are brought together, bring your hands down from your chest, one over the other, into the "ready" position.

25

BUNKAI NO. 25

B: Complete the morote tsuki. A: Maintain the posture of the preceding photograph (that is, left kihondachi stance, left arm extended).

BUNKAI NO. 26

Prepare for the ending formality. A: Pivot clockwise slightly on your right foot and bring your left back into a musubidachi stance. Close your hands. B: Move out of the left zenkutsu dachi stance by stepping back slightly with your left foot toward a center line even with A's. Then, slide your right foot toward this center line into the musubidachi position. Close your hands.

BUNKAI NO. 27

Both A and B: From the closing hands position, assume the ready position of the ending formality sequence.

25

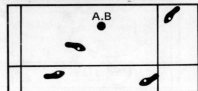

A.B

KATA NOS. 28—30

On completing the closing position, as shown in No. 26, and the ready position, as shown in No. 27, lower your arms to your sides and end the kata with the (28) attention, (29) bowing and (30) attention sequence of the ending formality.

28

BUNKAI NOS. 28—30

Both **A** and **B**: Complete the ending formality sequence of (28) attention, (29) bowing, and (30) a return to the attention stance.

28

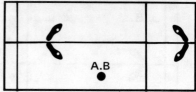

A.B

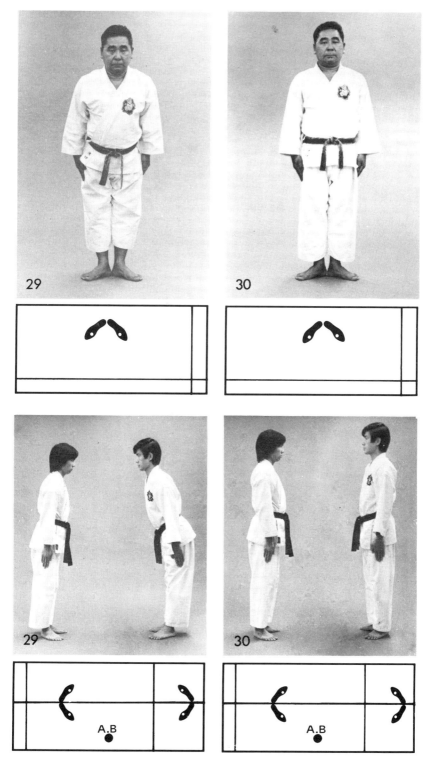

29

30

29

A.B

30

A.B

KISO KUMITE NO. 1

In conjunction with Hookiyu Kata No. 1 and its Bunkai, the student at the first grade or level studies Kiso Kumite No. 1.

Kiso Kumite No. 1 consists of six sets of techniques, with six techniques in each set. The first four techniques or movements in all six sets are the same and consist, very simply, of stepping, punching and blocking. The sets differ only in the last two movements presented in each.

As before, figure "A" is on the left, figure "B" is on the right. Students should practice both the "A" and "B" positions in all six sets.

The following techniques, previously discussed, are presented in Kiso Kumite No. 1:

Walking:	basic walking
Punching:	basic high punch (jodan tsuki)
	basic middle punch (chudan tsuki)
	basic low punch (gedan tsuki)
Blocking:	basic high block (jodan uke)
	basic middle block (chudan uke)
	basic low block (gedan uke)

Age Tsuki
Yoko Kentsui Uchi

SIDE VIEW   SIDE VIEW

NEW TECHNIQUES INTRODUCED

There are two new techniques introduced in Kiso Kumite No. 1 — YOKO KENTSUI UCHI or hammer punch to the temple and AGE TSUKI or upper cut.

YOKO KENTSUI UCHI
(HAMMER PUNCH TO THE TEMPLE)

(1) To strike with a left-hand hammer punch, begin in the kamae or on-guard position, right hand forward. (2) Bring your left fist, knuckles to the back

SIDE VIEW

SIDE VIEW

and thumb down, to a point near your left ear. Pull your elbow up and back until it is even with your shoulders. This movement should open your chest wide. (3) To punch, swing your arm forward, twisting your wrist counterclockwise as you go for your opponent's temple. (4) The blow should fall with the outside edge of your clenched left fist, knuckles toward the floor. Remember to keep your wrists straight.

To strike with your right hand, repeat the above. However, twist your wrist clockwise, not counterclockwise, as the blow lands.

AGE TSUKI
(UPPER CUT)

To execute an age tsuki or upper cut with your left hand, (1) from the kamae or on-guard position, right hand forward, (2-3) bring your left fist, palm toward the ceiling, straight up toward the head or chin of your opponent. Simultaneously, withdraw your right hand. Keep the blow moving on a straight line; do not let it curve as in a boxer's upper cut. Again, remember to keep your wrists straight. As with other punches, primary contact is made with the knuckles of your first two fingers.

A right age tsuki is delivered in the same manner but withdraw your left hand as the right strikes.

SIDE VIEW

2

3

SIDE VIEW

SIDE VIEW

85

SET I

(1) Both **A** and **B**: Face each other in a right kamae or on-guard stance. (2) **A**: Step forward with your left foot into a left kihondachi stance and execute a left jodan (high) punch. **B**: Step backward with your right foot into a left kihondachi stance. Stop **A**'s left jodan punch with a left jodan (high) block. (3) **A**: Step forward again, this time with your right foot, into a right kihondachi stance. As you do so, shoot out a right chudan (middle) punch. **B**: As **A** advances, move back with your left foot into a right kihondachi stance and counter **A**'s punch with a right chudan (middle) block. (4) **A**: Continue your advance, stepping forward into a left kihondachi stance and strike toward **B** with a left gedan (low) punch. **B**: Retreat by stepping back with your right foot into a left kihondachi stance. Protect yourself from **A**'s left gedan punch by executing a left gedan (low) block. (5) **A**: Step forward into a right kihondachi stance and execute a right jodan (high) punch. **B**: Pivot clockwise slightly on your right foot and step backward with your left some forty-five degrees into a shikodachi stance. By doing so, you evade **A**'s right jodan punch. Keep your left arm down and extended toward the level of your navel, your right withdrawn, as at the end of the left gedan block in No. 4. (6) **B**: Without changing your stance, shoot a right punch straight out toward **A**'s stomach (gedan punch). **A**: Having completed a right jodan punch, do not move but maintain your position (that is, right arm extended at shoulder level, or toward the level of your mouth, feet in a right kihondachi stance).

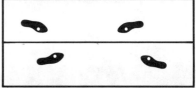

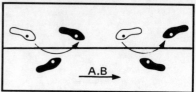

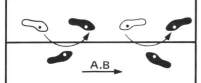

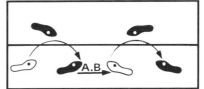

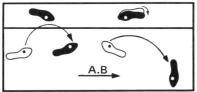

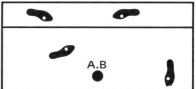

SET II

(1) Both **A** and **B**: Face each other in a right kamae or on-guard stance. (2) **A**: Step forward with your left foot into a left kihondachi stance and execute a left jodan (high) punch. **B**: Step backward with your right foot into a left kihondachi stance. Stop **A**'s left jodan punch with a left jodan (high) block. (3) **A**: Step forward again, this time with your right foot, into a right kihondachi stance. As you do so, shoot out a right chudan (middle) punch. **B**: As **A** advances, move back with your left foot into a right kihondachi stance and counter **A**'s punch with a right chudan (middle) block. (4) **A**: Continue your advance, stepping forward into a left kihondachi stance and strike toward **B** with a left gedan (low) punch. **B**: Retreat by stepping back with your right foot into a left kihondachi stance. Protect yourself from **A**'s left gedan punch by executing a left gedan (low) block. (5) **A**: Step forward into a right kihondachi stance, executing a right chudan (middle) punch as you do so. **B**: Step back with your left foot into a right kihondachi stance and counter **A**'s punch with a right chudan (middle) block. (6) **B**: Keep your feet in the right kihondachi stance and strike toward **A** with a left chudan (middle) punch. **A**: On completing the right chudan punch, do not move but maintain your position (that is, right arm extended toward the level of your solar plexus, left arm withdrawn, feet in a right kihondachi stance).

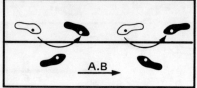

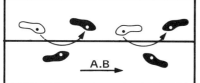

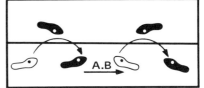

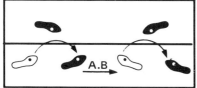

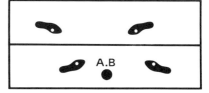

SET III

(1) Both **A** and **B**: Face each other in a right kamae or on-guard stance. (2) **A**: Step forward with your left foot into a left kihondachi stance and execute a left jodan (high) punch. **B**: Step backward with your right foot into a left kihondachi stance. Stop **A**'s left jodan punch with a left jodan (high) block. (3) **A**: Step forward again, this time with your right foot, into a right kihondachi stance. As you do so, shoot out a right chudan (middle) punch. **B**: As **A** advances, move back with your left foot into a right kihondachi stance and counter **A**'s punch with a right chudan (middle) block. (4) **A**: Continue your advance, stepping forward into a left kihondachi stance and strike toward **B** with a left gedan (low) punch. **B**: Retreat by stepping back with your right foot into a left kihondachi stance. Protect yourself from **A**'s left gedan punch by executing a left gedan (low) block. (5) **A**: Step forward with your right foot into a right kihondachi stance. As you do so, execute a right gedan (low) punch. **B**: As **A** steps forward, step back with your left foot into a right kihondachi position. Hold off **A**'s punch with a right gedan (low) block. (6) **B**: Complete a left hammer punch (yoko kentsui uchi) near **A**'s right temple. Do not move your feet but keep them in the right kihondachi position. **A**: Having executed a right gedan punch, maintain your position (that is, right arm extended toward the level of your navel, left arm withdrawn, feet in a right kihondachi stance).

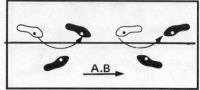

90

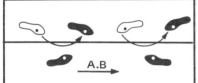

2

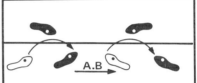

3

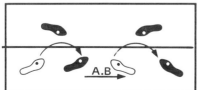

5

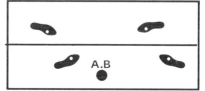

6

SET IV

(1) Both **A** and **B**: Face each other in a right kamae or on-guard stance.
(2) **A**: Step forward with your left foot into a left kihondachi stance and execute a left jodan (high) punch. **B**: Step backward with your right foot into a left kihondachi stance. Stop **A**'s left jodan punch with a left jodan (high) block.
(3) **A**: Step forward again, this time with your right foot, into a right kihondachi stance. As you do so, shoot out a right chudan (middle) punch. **B**: As **A** advances, move back with your left foot into a right kihondachi stance and counter **A**'s punch with a right chudan (middle) block.
(4) **A**: Continue your advance, stepping forward into a left kihondachi stance and strike toward **B** with a left gedan (low) punch. **B**: Retreat by stepping back with your right foot into a left kihondachi stance. Protect yourself from **A**'s left gedan punch by executing a left gedan (low) block. (5) **A**: As you step forward with your right foot into a right kihondachi stance, complete a right jodan (high) punch. **B**: Step backward with your left foot into a right kihondachi stance and block **A**'s punch with a right jodan uke (high block).
(6) **B**: Do not move your feet as you strike toward **A** with a left chudan (middle) punch. **A**: Maintain the position you assumed at the end of your right jodan punch (that is, right arm extended at head level, left arm withdrawn, feet in a right kihondachi stance).

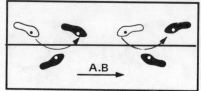

2

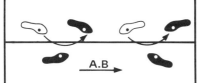

3

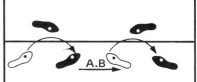

5

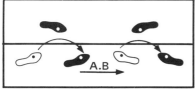

6

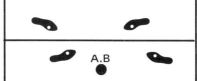

SET V

(1) Both **A** and **B**: Face each other in a right kamae or on-guard stance. (2) **A**: Step forward with your left foot into a left kihondachi stance and execute a left jodan (high) punch. **B**: Step backward with your right foot into a left kihondachi stance. Stop **A**'s left jodan punch with a left jodan (high) block. (3) **A**: Step forward again, this time with your right foot, into a right kihondachi stance. As you do so, shoot out a right chudan (middle) punch. **B**: As **A** advances, move back with your left foot into a right kihondachi stance and counter **A**'s punch with a right chudan (middle) block. (4) **A**: Continue your advance, stepping forward into a left kihondachi stance and strike toward **B** with a left gedan (low) punch. **B**: Retreat by stepping back with your right foot into a left kihondachi stance. Protect yourself from **A**'s left gedan punch by executing a left gedan (low) block. (5) **A**: Step forward with your right foot into a right kihondachi stance and shoot out a right chudan (middle) punch. **B**: Step back with your left foot into a right kihondachi stance and protect yourself with a right chudan (middle) block. (6) **B**: Without stepping in any direction, direct a left punch toward **A**'s right eye (jodan tsuki). **A**: Maintain the position you assumed at the end of the right chudan punch in No. 5 (that is, right arm extended at the level of your solar plexus, left arm withdrawn, feet in a right kihondachi position).

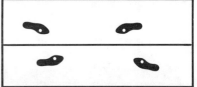

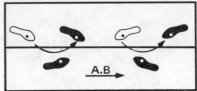

2

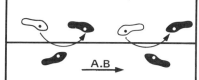

A.B

3

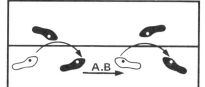

A.B

5

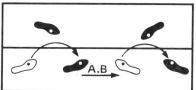

A.B

6

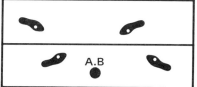

A.B

SET VI

(1) Both **A** and **B**: Face each other in a right kamae or on-guard stance. (2) **A**: Step forward with your left foot into a left kihondachi stance and execute a left jodan (high) punch. **B**: Step backward with your right foot into a left kihondachi stance. Stop **A**'s left jodan punch with a left jodan (high) block. (3) **A**: Step forward again, this time with your right foot, into a right kihondachi stance. As you do so, shoot out a right chudan (middle) punch. **B**: As **A** advances, move back with your left foot into a right kihondachi stance and counter **A**'s punch with a right chudan (middle) block. (4) **A**: Continue your advance, stepping forward into a left kihondachi stance and strike toward **B** with a left gedan (low) punch. **B**: Retreat by stepping back with your right foot into a left kihondachi stance. Protect yourself from **A**'s left gedan punch by executing a left gedan (low) block. (5) **A**: Execute a right gedan (low) punch as you step forward with your right foot into a right kihondachi stance. **B**: As **A** moves toward you, step back with your left foot into a right kihondachi position and shield yourself with a right gedan (low) block. (6) **B**: Strike toward **A** with a left upper cut (age tsuki) to his chin. Do not step out of place. **A**: Upon execution of your right gedan punch (No. 5), maintain your position (that is, right arm extended down toward the level of your navel, left arm withdrawn, feet in a right kihondachi position).

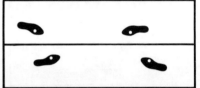

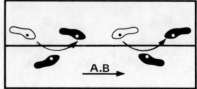

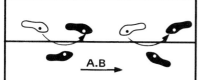

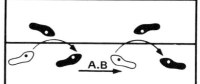

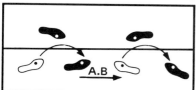

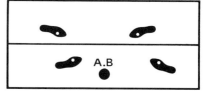

KISO KUMITE NO. 2

As mentioned earlier, although Hookiyu Kata No. 1 (grade 1) should be followed by Hookiyu Kata No. 2 (grade 2), the latter will not be included in this text because it so closely resembles the former. The Kiso Kumite No. 2 from grade 2, however, is presented and the judicious student will master this exercise before proceeding on to Gekisai No. 1 (from grade 3). The Kiso Kumite for Gekisai No. 1 will be introduced at a later date in another text.

Kiso Kumite No. 2 consists of six sets of techniques with five techniques in each set. Each set of techniques has been designated first, second, third, etc. The student should study the sets in this order. As before, he is also advised to practice the roles of both A and B.

The techniques used in Kiso Kumite No. 2 are as follows:

Walking:	basic walking and sliding
Punching:	basic jodan, chudan and gedan
Blocking:	basic jodan, chudan and gedan
Others:	age tsuki
	mae shuto uchi
	soko tsuki

SIDE VIEW   SIDE VIEW

NEW TECHNIQUES INTRODUCED

There are two new techniques introduced in Kiso Kumite No. 2 — MAE SHUTO UCHI or front chop strike and SOKO TSUKI or under cut.

MAE SHUTO UCHI (FRONT CHOP STRIKE)

(1) Begin in the kamae or on-guard position, right foot and hand forward. To strike with your left, (2) bring your left elbow up and back to a level even with your shoulder and your left hand, open and palm facing forward, to a point above your ear. (3-4) To execute the blow, sweep your arm out in front of you, twisting it counterclockwise to hit the target with the outer edge of

3

4

SIDE VIEW

SIDE VIEW

your hand (as indicated in the diagram). Your target is usually your opponent's neck. When the mae shuto uchi lands, the palm of your hand should face upwards.

To strike with your right hand, repeat the above but twist your hand clockwise, not counterclockwise, as it comes forward to chop.

SOKO TSUKI
(UNDER CUT)

To execute a soko tsuki (under cut), (1) pull your elbow and striking fist, palm toward the ceiling, straight back keeping your forearm on a level parallel to the floor and even with your solar plexus. Shoot your fist straight out, usually to your opponent's stomach, lower abdomen or groin. (2) As you hit the target, curve your fist upward so that the blow

SIDE VIEW

2

lands with your lower knuckles (as indicated in the diagram). When using the soko tsuki, you should be able to strike the target without fully extending your arm. In fact, do not extend your elbow/arm to deliver the blow as this diminishes its effectiveness. On completing the movement, withdraw your striking fist as quickly as possible.

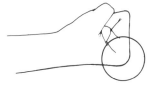

SIDE VIEW

SET I

(1) Both **A** and **B**: Face each other in a right kamae or on-guard position. (2) **A**: Step forward with your left foot into a left kihondachi stance, striking toward **B** with a left jodan (high) punch as you do so. **B**: Counter **A**'s blow with a left jodan (high) block while stepping backward on your right foot into a left kihondachi stance. (3) **B**: Strike toward **A** with a right gedan (low) punch. At this point, do not step out of the left kihondachi stance. **A**: Do not move your feet out of their left kihondachi stance, either. They will remain in this position through Nos. 3-5. Protect yourself from **B** with a left gedan (low) block. (4) **A**: Move out of the left gedan (low) block and complete a right gedan (low) punch. **B**: Keep your feet stationary and block to the low left (gedan block). (5) **B**: Keep your left arm in a gedan (low) block. Slide forward approximately 2.0 S on your left foot and 1.0 S on your right. Pivot counterclockwise on your right foot into a left sho zenkutsu dachi stance. As you assume this position, execute a right gedan (low) punch. **A**: Maintain your previous position.

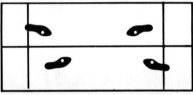

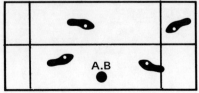

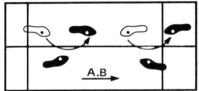

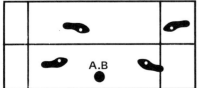

SET II

(1) Both **A** and **B:** Face each other in a right kamae or on-guard position. (2) **A:** Step forward with your left foot into a left kihondachi stance, striking toward **B** with a left chudan (middle) punch as you do so. **B:** Counter **A**'s blow with a left chudan (middle) block while stepping back on your right foot into a left kihondachi stance. (3) **B:** Strike toward **A** with a right chudan (middle) punch. At this point, do not step out of the left kihondachi stance. **A:** Do not move your feet out of their left kihondachi stance either. They will remain in this position through Nos. 3-5. Protect yourself from **B** with a left chudan (middle) block. (4) **A:** Move out of the left chudan block and complete a right chudan (middle) punch. **B:** Keep your feet stationary and block to the middle left (chudan block). (5) **B:** Grab **A**'s right sleeve with your left hand. Slide forward approximately 2.0 S on your left foot and 1.0 S on your right. Pivot counterclockwise on your right foot into a left sho zenkutsu dachi stance. As you assume this position, execute a right chudan (middle) punch. **A:** Maintain your previous position.

1

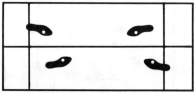

3

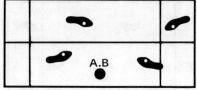

2

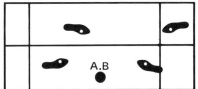

4

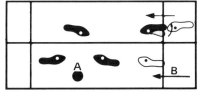

5

1

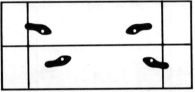

SET III

(1) Both **A** and **B**: Face each other in a right kamae or on-guard position. (2) **A**: Step forward with your left foot into a left kihondachi stance, striking toward **B** with a left gedan (low) punch as you do so. **B**: Counter **A**'s blow with a left gedan (low) block while stepping backward on your right foot into a left kihondachi stance. (3) **B**: Strike toward **A** with a right jodan (high) punch. At this point, do not step out of the left kihondachi stance. **A**: Do not move your feet out of their left kihondachi stance, either. They will remain in this position through Nos. 3-5. Protect yourself from **B** with a left jodan (high) block. (4) **A**: Move out of the left jodan block and complete a right jodan (high) punch. B Keep your feet stationary and block to the high left (jodan block). (5) **B**: Keep your left arm in a left jodan (high) block. Slide forward approximately 2.0 S on your left foot and 1.0 S on your right. Pivot counterclockwise on your right foot into a left sho zenkutsu dachi stance. As you assume this position, execute a right jodan (high) punch to **A**'s chin. **A**: Maintain your previous position.

3

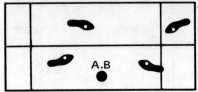

2

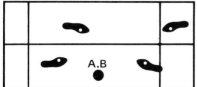

A.B

4

A.B

5

A

B

SET IV

(1) Both **A** and **B**: Face each other in a right kamae or on-guard position. (2) **A**: Step forward with your left foot into a left kihondachi stance, striking toward **B** with a left jodan (high) punch as you do so. **B**: Counter **A**'s blow with a left jodan (high) block while stepping back on your right foot into a left kihondachi stance. (3) **B**: Strike toward **A** with a right chudan (middle) punch. At this point, do not step out of the left kihondachi stance. **A**: Do not move your feet out of their left kihondachi stance, either. They will remain in this position through Nos. 3-5. Although you should technically protect yourself from **B** with a left chudan (middle) block, in this particular case, use a block to the low left (gedan block). (4) **A**: Move out of the left gedan block and complete a right chudan (middle) punch. **B**: Keep your feet stationary and block to the middle left (chudan block). (5) **B**: Slide forward approximately 2.0 S on your left foot and 1.0 S on your right. Pivot counterclockwise on your right foot into a left sho zenkutsu dachi stance. As you assume this position, grab **A**'s left sleeve with your left hand and execute a right soko tsuki (under cut) to **A**'s lower ribs. **A**: Maintain your previous position.

1

3

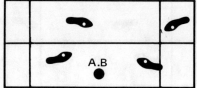

2

4

5

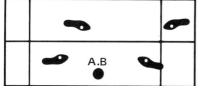

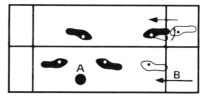

1

SET V

(1) Both **A** and **B:** Face each other in a right kamae or on-guard position. (2) **A:** Step forward with your left foot into a left kihondachi stance, striking toward **B** with a left chudan (middle) punch as you do so. **B:** Block **A**'s blow with a left chudan (middle) block while stepping back on your right foot into a left kihondachi stance. (3) **B:** Strike toward **A** with a right jodan (high) punch. At this point, do not step out of the left kihondachi stance. **A:** Do not move your feet out of their left kihondachi stance, either. They will remain in this position through Nos. 3-5. Protect yourself from **B** with a left jodan (high) block. (4) **A:** Move out of the left jodan (high) block and complete a right jodan (high) punch. **B:** Keep your feet stationary and block to the high left (jodan block). (5) **B:** Keep your left arm in a jodan (high) block. Slide forward approximately 2.0 S on your left foot and 1.0 S on your right. Pivot counterclockwise on your right foot into a left sho zenkutsu dachi stance. As you assume this position, execute a right mae shuto uchi (front chop strike) to **A**'s neck. **A:** Maintain your previous position.

3

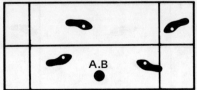

2

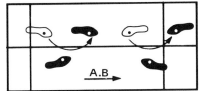

A.B

4

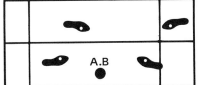

A.B

5

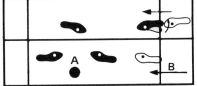

A

B

113

SET VI

(1) Both **A** and **B**: Face each other in a right kamae or on-guard position. (2) **A**: Step forward with your left foot into a left kihondachi stance, striking toward **B** with a left gedan (low) punch as you do so. **B**: Counter **A**'s blow with a left gedan (low) block while stepping back on your right foot into a left kihondachi stance. (3) **B**: Strike toward **A** with a right jodan (high) punch. At this point, do not step out of the left kihondachi stance. **A**: Do not move your feet out of their left kihondachi stance, either. They will remain in this position through Nos. 3-5. Protect yourself from **B** with a left jodan (high) block. (4) **A**: Move out of the left jodan block and complete a right jodan (high) punch. **B**: Keep your feet stationary and block to the high left (jodan block). (5) **B**: Keep your left arm in a jodan block. Slide forward approximately 2.0 S on your left foot and 1.0 S on your right. Pivot counterclockwise on your right foot into a left sho zenkutsu dachi stance. As you assume this position, execute a right age tsuki (upper cut) to **A**'s chin. **A**: Maintain your previous position.

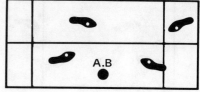

114

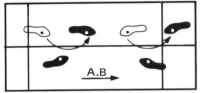

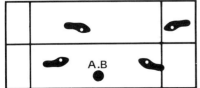

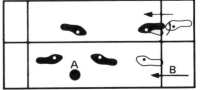

GEKISAI NO. 1 KATA AND BUNKAI

At the third grade or level, the student learns Gekisai No. 1 Kata. Then, with a partner, he studies the corresponding bunkai (Bunkai Kumite No. 3—see page 20). As before, the movements of the kata and the bunkai have been set up in parallel sequence. Remember, however, kata should be perfected *before* moving on to the bunkai.

1

NEW TECHNIQUES INTRODUCED

There are three techniques introduced in Gekisai No. 1 Kata — SHOMEN GERI (front kick), TATE EMPI (elbow attack) and URAKEN UCHI (back fist strike).

Shomen geri and tate empi are used in combination and a blocking sequence to counter this combination is also presented.

SHOMEN GERI
(FRONT KICK)

To execute a front kick with your right foot, (1) begin in the musubi-dachi stance, hands on hips. (2) Bend your right knee and bring it up in front of you around the level of your belt. When raised in this position, your right foot should be roughly parallel to the floor, in line with your right knee and pulled in slightly. As you lift your right knee, let your left leg bend only slightly to put spring in the kick. Keep your head and torso erect. (3) To kick, shoot your right foot out, straightening your knee on

2

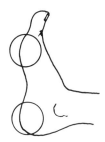

3

a level even with and in front of your groin. Execute the kick in somewhat of a flat-footed manner (that is, with your heel out). Although you should hit your target with the ball of your foot, on occasion, the heel is also used to make primary contact (see diagram). In either case, do not point your toes. After the kick has been completed, (4) withdraw your right foot as quickly as possible, returning to the "ready" position (knee up and cocked).

To execute a left front kick, repeat the above, reversing right and left.

4

TATE EMPI
(ELBOW ATTACK)

To execute a strike with your right elbow, (1) begin in the right zenkutsu dachi stance with your left arm extended, right arm withdrawn, as at the end of a left gedan (low) punch. (2-3) Bring your right fist, palm inward, over your right shoulder. Swiftly move your elbow up to hit the target on a level even with your solar plexus. As your elbow moves to make contact, slightly twist your right shoulder into, and your left shoulder away from the target to give more force to the blow. When the attack has been completed, your right elbow and arm should be even and on the same plane as your shoul-

2

ders. Remember, from the "ready" position through the attack, your right fist should remain close to your right shoulder. As your right elbow begins the attack, pull your left fist toward your left armpit, twisting it counterclockwise so your palm faces the ceiling instead of the floor. This movement should tie in smoothly with the twist of your left shoulder as you make contact with the target. Keep your left elbow down and to the back.

To execute a strike with your left elbow, reverse right and left in the directions given above. Twist your right fist clockwise as it is withdrawn.

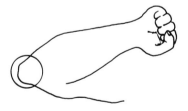

3

1

SHOMEN GERI/TATE EMPI (FRONT KICK/ELBOW ATTACK) COMBINATION

Beginning with your arms in a left kamae position and your feet in a musubidachi stance, (1) execute a shomen geri (front kick) with your right foot. (2) On completing the

2

kick, (3) return to the "ready" position and (4) step smoothly with your right foot into a right zenkutsu dachi stance. As you do so, execute a right tate empi (elbow attack).

SHOMEN GERI/TATE EMPI COMBINATION BLOCKING SEQUENCE

Blocking a shomen geri/tate empi (front kick/elbow attack) combination involves using gedan (low) blocks and palm blocks. (1) To counter a left shomen geri/left tate empi combination, move away as quickly as possible into a left zenkutsu dachi stance. Simultaneously, put down a right gedan (low) block to stop your opponent's left shomen geri (front kick). At this point, your opponent will withdraw his left leg and commence execution of a left tate empi (elbow attack). When he does so, (2) bring your left hand, open with palm toward him, forward over your solar plexus. Do not let your left hand rest against your body but hold it a few inches away from your torso. (3) As your opponent's elbow begins moving up to hit your solar plexus, bring your right fist, palm toward the ceiling, up toward your right armpit, keeping your right elbow down and to the back. At the same time, pivot clockwise on the balls of both feet into a right zenbutsu dachi stance and stop his elbow with your left hand (left palm block). While pivoting, keep your head and eyes turned toward the on-coming blow, not away from it.

To protect yourself from a right shomen geri/right tate empi combination, repeat the instructions given above, reversing right and left (that is, use a left gedan block/right zenkutsu dachi and a right palm block/-counterclockwise pivot to a left zenkutsu dachi sequence). To facilitate smooth execution of this blocking sequence, practice pivoting quickly into both the right and left zenbutsu dachi positions.

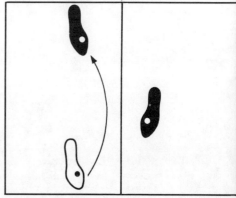

2

3

URAKEN UCHI
(BACK FIST STRIKE)

To complete a back fist strike (uraken uchi) with your right hand, (1-2) bring your right fist, palm facing the floor, up toward your right ear, pulling your right elbow up and back, even with your shoulders (as in the hammer punch). (3) Swing your arm down, dropping your elbow into the blow and hit your target (usually your opponent's chin) with the back of your hand. Primary contact

should come from the area around your middle knuckles (see diagram). Keep your wrist loose to facilitate a sharp snap down, then up, into the target, as the blow connects. (4) After the strike has been completed, do not continue dropping your right elbow but bring it upward with a snap also. A back fist strike with your left hand is executed in much the same manner.

3

4

1

KATA NOS. 1—3

Execute the beginning formality sequence of (1) attention, (2) bowing, and (3) a return to attention.

BUNKAI NOS.1—3

Both **A** and **B**: Execute the beginning formality sequence of (1) attention, (2) bowing, and (3) a return to attention.

1

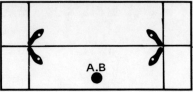

A.B

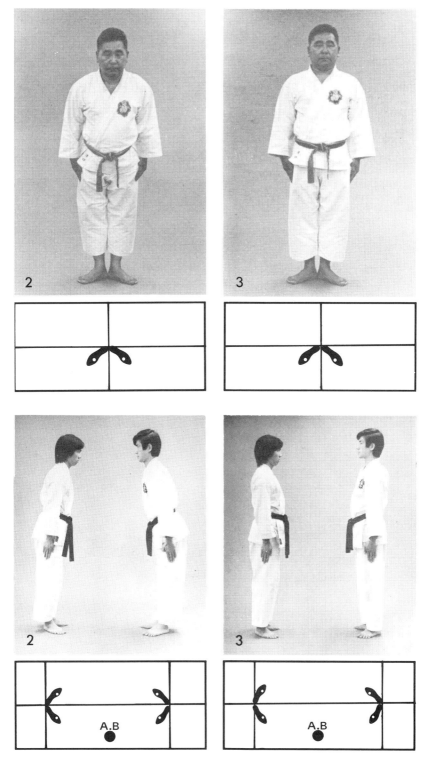

KATA NOS. 4—6

Complete the beginning formality sequence of (4) ready, (5) opening, and finally, (6) right on-guard or kamae stance.

4

BUNKAI NOS. 4—6

Both **A** and **B**: Complete the beginning formality sequence of (4) ready, (5) opening, and (6) right on-guard or kamae stance.

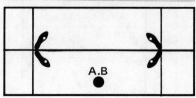

4

A.B

130

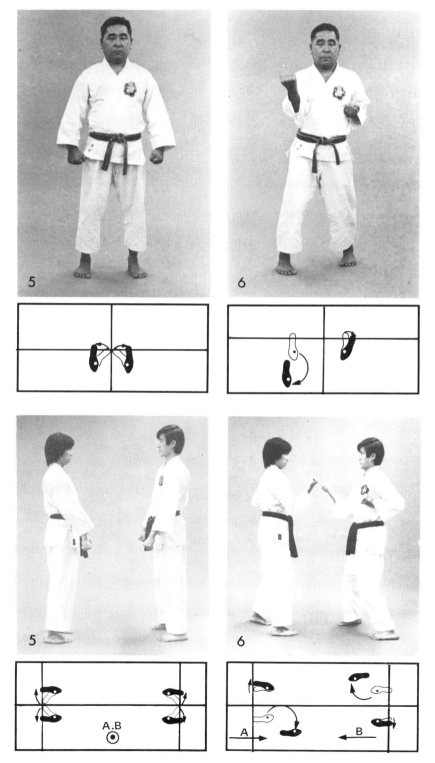

KATA NO. 7
From the kamae or on-guard position, slide your right foot .5 S on a line parallel to enbusen line AD. Now, pivot counterclockwise on both feet into a kihondachi stance in the direction of enbusen line D. From a kihondachi position where your right foot is forward, you will have moved into a kihondachi stance with your left foot forward (as in Hookiyu Kata I, No. 7). On completing the pivot, put up a left jodan (high) block.

KATA NO. 8
As you step forward with your right foot into a right kihondachi stance, execute a right chudan (middle) punch.

KATA NO. 9
Swing your right foot back and to your right (in the direction of enbusen line C). As you do so, pivot clockwise on your left foot into a shikodachi stance, placing both heels along enbusen line CD. Simultaneously, execute a left gedan (low) block. Keep your eyes and head turned to your left (in the direction of enbusen line D and toward the imaginary oncoming punch).

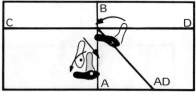

BUNKAI NO. 7
B: Step toward A with your left foot and execute a left jodan (high) punch. A: Step backward with your right foot into a left kihondachi stance. Block to the high left (jodan block).

BUNKAI NO. 8
A: Step forward with your right foot and throw a right chudan (middle) punch. B: In response to A's attack, step backward with your left foot and protect yourself with a right chudan (middle) block.

BUNKAI NO. 9
B: From the right kihondachi stance, pivot clockwise on your right foot, stepping forward with your left forty-five degrees into a shikodachi stance. As you step forward, execute a left gedan (low) punch. A: From your right kihondachi stance, pivot counterclockwise slightly on your left foot, stepping back with your right forty-five degrees into a shikodachi position. As you step back, stop B's blow with a left gedan (low) block.

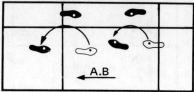

KATA NO. 10

Move out of the shikodachi stance by pivoting clockwise on your right foot as you bring your left toward it into a right kihondachi stance in the direction of enbusen line C. At the same time, put up a right jodan (high) block.

KATA NO. 11

Step forward with your left foot in the direction of enbusen line C, throwing a chudan (middle) punch with your left hand.

KATA NO. 12

Swing your left foot back and to your left (in the direction of enbusen line D). As you do so, pivot counterclockwise slightly on your right foot, moving into a shikodachi stance with both heels along enbusen line CD. As your feet move into the shikodachi stance, execute a right gedan (low) block, keeping your head and eyes to the right in the direction of enbusen line C (or toward the imaginary oncoming gedan punch).

BUNKAI NO. 10

A: Pivot clockwise slightly on your left foot and step forward with your right, moving out of the shikodachi position back into your original right kihondachi stance. Strike toward **B** with a right jodan (high) punch. **B:** Move out of the shikodachi position back into your original right kihondachi stance by pivoting counterclockwise on your right foot and stepping back with your left. As you do so, counter **A**'s punch with a right jodan (high) block.

BUNKAI NO. 11

B: Step forward with your left foot and throw out a left chudan (middle) punch. **A:** Step back with your right foot and put up a left chudan (middle) block.

BUNKAI NO. 12

A: Pivot counterclockwise on your left foot, stepping forward with your right foot forty-five degrees into a second shikodachi stance. Complete with a right gedan (low) punch. **B:** Pivot clockwise slightly on your right foot. Stepping back on your left at a forty-five degree angle into a second shikodachi stance, block **A**'s right punch with a right gedan (low) block.

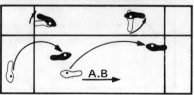

KATA NO. 13

From the shikodachi stance, pivot counter-clockwise slightly on your right foot. Step with your left into a left kihondachi stance in the direction of enbusen line A. As your feet shift, slowly throw up a left chudan (middle) block.

NOTE: As in Hookiyu Kata I, No. 13, do not forget to slide your left foot forward past your right in a semi-circular manner when you take the step.

KATA NO. 14

Step forward with your right foot into a right kihondachi stance. Withdraw your left hand and slowly move into a chudan (middle) block with your right.

KATA NO. 15

Pivot clockwise on your right foot as you bring your left knee up in preparation for a left shomen geri (front kick). Keep your hands as they were at the end of your right chudan block.

BUNKAI NO. 13

B: Return to the left kihondachi stance by pivoting counterclockwise slightly on your right foot as you step forward with your left. Complete a left chudan (middle) punch to A's chest. A: Pivot clockwise on your left foot, step back on your right and return to a left kihondachi stance. Protect yourself from B with a left chudan (middle) block.

BUNKAI NO. 14

B: Step forward with your right into a right kihondachi position and strike toward A's solar plexus with a right chudan (middle) punch. A: Step backward with your left into a right kihondachi stance as you execute a right chudan (middle) block.

BUNKAI NO. 15

A: Assume the shomen geri (front kick) "ready" position by pivoting clockwise on your right foot and bringing your left up in front of you. Your arms should remain as they were at the end of the chudan block. A shomen geri/tate empi (front kick/elbow attack) combination begins here. B: Maintain the right kihondachi stance, keeping your right arm extended, left arm withdrawn, as at the end of the chudan punch.

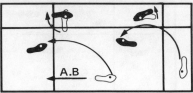

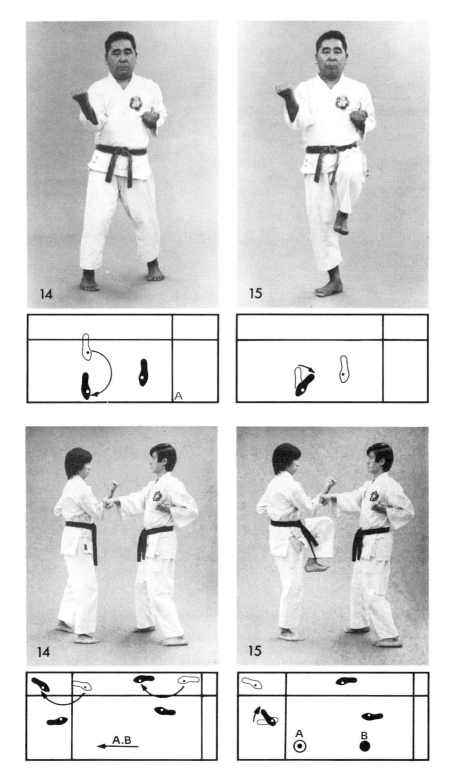

KATA NO. 16

Execute the left shomen geri (front kick) as previously discussed. Do not move your hands.

KATA NO. 17

On completing the kick, withdraw your left foot. Keep your knee up, however, until you begin moving into the next technique.

KATA NO. 18

Pivot counterclockwise on your right foot as you simultaneously stamp your left down into a left zenkutsu dachi position. Bring your right arm back, raise your left fist to your left shoulder and strike toward your opponent with .a left tate empi (elbow attack) to the solar plexus.

After the tate empi (elbow attack) has been completed, do not lower your left arm but keep your fist held over your left shoulder. Twist your fist so that the back of your hand faces your target in readiness for a left uraken uchi (back fist strike).

16

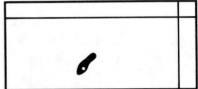

BUNKAI NO. 16

A: Complete a left shomen geri (front kick). B: Slide your right foot back into a left zenkutsu dachi stance. Keep your left foot stationary. Begin a shomen geri/tate empi blocking sequence by executing a right gedan (low) block.

BUNKAI NO. 17

A: Return your left foot to the "ready" position. Do not step down with it into another kihondachi stance. B: Keep your arms and feet as they were at the end of the right gedan block.

BUNKAI NO. 18

A: Pivot counterclockwise on your right foot and stamp down with your left into a left zenkutsu dachi stance. As you do so, bring your right arm back, pull your left fist over your left shoulder and swiftly thrust a left tate empi (elbow attack) toward B's solar plexus. Do not drop your elbow after striking but prepare for a left uraken uchi (back fist strike). B: Pivoting clockwise on the balls of both feet, turn ninety degrees into a right zenkutsu dachi stance. Stop A's left tate empi with a left palm block. Withdraw your right fist as your left blocks.

16

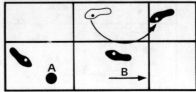

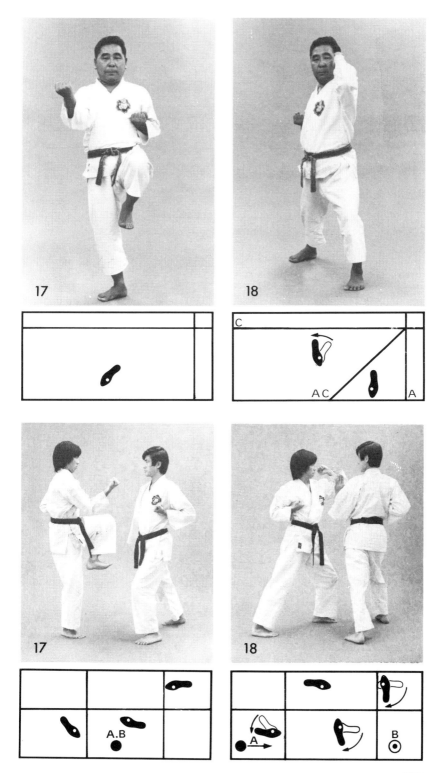

KATA NO. 19

Shifting only your left arm, smoothly move your up-raised fist from the completed left tate empi down swiftly into a left uraken uchi (back fist strike) near your opponent's chin. In all other respects, maintain the stance and posture of the preceding photograph.

KATA NO. 20

Execute a left gedan (low) block. Do not move out of the left zenkutsu dachi stance.

KATA NO. 21

Twist your torso counterclockwise (that is, back toward enbusen line A). Move from the left gedan block to a right gedan (low) punch. Continue to maintain the left zenkutsu dachi stance.

19

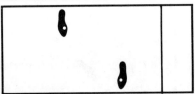

BUNKAI NO. 19

A: While in the left zenkutsu dachi position, keep your right fist tucked near your right armpit and bring your left down out of the tate empi (elbow attack) into a uraken uchi (back fist strike) near B's chin. B: As A's uraken uchi comes down toward your chin, use the left palm block to push his left arm away and thereby, neutralize the blow. Throughout this, your feet remain in the right zenkutsu dachi stance.

BUNKAI NO. 20

B: Pivot counterclockwise on both feet, turning ninety degrees to face A in a left zenkutsu dachi stance. Execute a right gedan (low) punch. A: Maintain the left zenkutsu dachi stance and block to the low left (gedan block).

BUNKAI NO. 21

A: Move out of the left gedan block into a right gedan (low) punch. Keep your feet in their left zenkutsu dachi stance. B: Protect yourself from A's punch with a left gedan (low) block. Your feet also remain in the left zenkutsu dachi stance.

19

KATA NO. 22

Prepare yourself for a right shuto uchi (side chop) in the direction of enbusen line B. Pivot clockwise slightly on your left foot, turn your head toward the target and sweep up your right foot. Your torso should now face in the direction of enbusen line C while your head is turned toward enbusen line B.

In accordance with your preliminary footwork, pull your left fist back, and bring your open right hand, palm to the ceiling, to your chest in the shuto uchi "ready" pose.

KATA NO. 23

Stamp your right foot down into a soto hachiji dachi position parallel to enbusen line AB as your right hand shoots out to deliver the shuto uchi (side chop) at neck level. Completing the chop should open your chest wide. Be sure to keep your head turned toward the target (in this case, in the direction of enbusen line B).

KATA NO. 24

Pivot clockwise on your right foot as you step with your left into a left kihondachi stance in the direction of enbusen line B. Slowly perform a chudan (middle) block to the left.

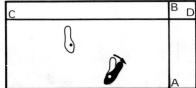

BUNKAI NO. 22

A: Assume the "ready" position for a left shuto uchi (side chop). Pivot clockwise ninety degrees on your right foot as you sweep your left up. Pull your right fist back. Bring your open left hand over your chest, palm toward the ceiling. **B:** Pivot clockwise ninety degrees into a right zenkutsu dachi stance. Pull your right fist back and prepare for a left jodan (high) block.

BUNKAI NO. 23

A: Stamp your left foot down into a soto hachiji dachi stance and strike toward **B**'s neck with the shuto uchi. Remember to open your chest wide as the chop is delivered. **B:** Protect yourself with the jodan block.

BUNKAI NO. 24

A: Just as you complete the shuto uchi, slide your left foot forward about 1.0 S. Then, step forward with your right (almost on top of **B**'s left) into a right kihondachi stance. Execute a right chudan (middle) punch. **B:** Slide your left foot back (before **A** steps on it) and pivot counterclockwise on your right into a right kihondachi stance. Put up a right chudan (middle) block.

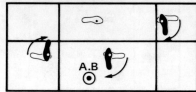

KATA NO. 25

Pivot counterclockwise some forty-five degrees on your left foot, lifting your right to the shomen geri (front kick) "ready" position. Keep your hands as they were at the end of the chudan block.

KATA NO. 26

Thrust your right foot out, executing the shomen geri. Again, keep your hands in position.

KATA NO. 27

After completing the kick, withdraw your right foot. Keep your knee up, however, until you begin moving into the next technique.

25

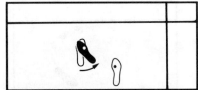

BUNKAI NO. 25

B: A second shomen geri/tate empi combination begins here. Pivot clockwise on your right foot and bring your left up into the shomen geri (front kick) "ready" position. Keep your hands in the completed right chudan (middle) block. A: Remain as you were at the end of the right chudan punch—that is, right arm extended, left withdrawn, feet in a right kihon-dachi position.

BUNKAI NO. 26

B: Keep your hands in place and complete the left shomen geri (front kick) at belt level. A: Step back on your right foot into a left zenkutsu dachi stance. As you do so, counter B's shomen geri with a block to the low right (gedan block). With this block, you begin a shomen geri/tate empi blocking sequence.

BUNKAI NO. 27

B: On completing the shomen geri (front kick), keep your hands in place and return your left foot to the "ready" position. Do not step with your left into another kihondachi stance. A: Remain in position keeping your arms as they were at the end of the right gedan block and your feet in a left zenkutsu dachi stance.

25

144

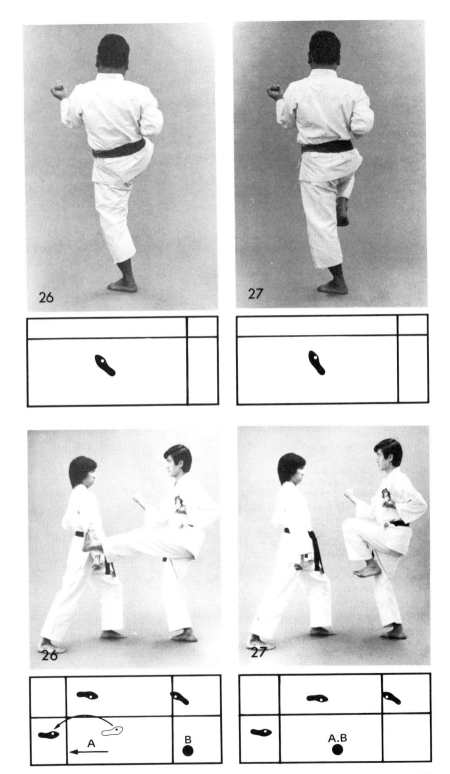

KATA NO. 28

Pivot clockwise on your left foot as you simultaneously stamp your right down into a right zenkutsu dachi position. Bring your left arm back, raise your right fist to your right shoulder and strike toward your opponent with a right tate empi (elbow attack).

After the tate empi has been completed, do not lower your right arm but keep your fist held over your right shoulder. Twist your fist so that the back of your hand faces your target in readiness for a right uraken uchi (back fist strike).

KATA NO. 29

Shifting only your right arm, smoothly move your up-raised fist from the completed right tate empi down swiftly into a right uraken uchi (back fist strike) near your opponent's chin. In all other respects, maintain the stance and posture of the preceding photograph.

KATA NO. 30

Execute a right gedan (low) block. Do not move out of the zenkutsu dachi stance.

28

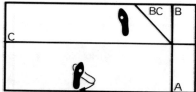

BUNKAI NO. 28

B: Pivot counterclockwise on your right foot and stamp down with your left into a left zenkutsu dachi stance. As you do so, bring your right arm back, pull your left fist over your left shoulder and swiftly thrust a left tate empi (elbow attack) toward **A**'s solar plexus. Do not drop your elbow after striking but prepare for a left uraken uchi (back fist strike). **A:** Pivoting clockwise on the balls of both feet, turn ninety degrees into a right zenkutsu dachi stance. Stop **B**'s left tate empi with a left palm block. Withdraw your right fist as your left blocks.

BUNKAI NO. 29

B: Keep your right fist tucked up near your right armpit. Bring your left down in a uraken uchi (back fist strike) near **A**'s chin. **A:** Neutralize **B**'s blow by using the left palm block to push his arm away.

BUNKAI NO. 30

A: Pivot counterclockwise ninety degrees on both feet, turning to face **B** in a left zenkutsu dachi stance. Strike toward him with a right gedan (low) punch. **B:** Counter with a left gedan (low) block.

28

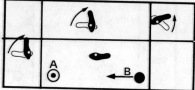

KATA NO. 31

Twist your torso forward (that is, back toward enbusen line B). Move from the right gedan block into a left gedan (low) punch. Continue to maintain the right zenkutsu dachi stance.

KATA NO. 32

Prepare yourself for a left shuto uchi (side chop) in the direction of enbusen line A. Pivot counterclockwise slightly on your right foot, turn your head toward the target and sweep up your left foot. Your torso should now face in the direction of enbusen line C while your head is turned toward enbusen line A.

In accordance with your preliminary footwork, pull your right fist back and bring your open left hand, palm to the ceiling, to your chest in the shuto uchi "ready" position.

KATA NO. 33

Stamp your left foot down into a soto hachiji dachi position parallel to enbusen line AB as your left hand shoots out in the shuto uchi (side chop) at neck level. Completing the chop should, as before, open your chest wide. Be sure to keep your head turned toward the target (that is, in the direction of enbusen line A).

BUNKAI NO. 31

B: Move from the left gedan block into a right gedan (low) punch. Your feet are stationary. **A:** Protect yourself from B's punch with a left gedan (low) block, keeping your feet in a left zenkutsu dachi stance.

BUNKAI NO. 32

B: Assume the "ready" position for a left shuto uchi (side chop) to A's neck by pivoting clockwise ninety degrees on your right foot as you sweep your left up. Pull your right fist back and bring your left hand, open with palm toward the ceiling, over your chest. **A:** Pivot clockwise ninety degrees on both feet, turning into a right zenkutsu dachi stance. Get ready to block to the high left (jodan block) by pulling your right fist back and preparing your left for its movement upward and outward.

BUNKAI NO. 33

B: Execute the shuto uchi to A's neck, stamping down with your left foot into a soto hachiji dachi stance. **A:** Stop B's shuto uchi with the left jodan block.

KATA NO. 34

From the soto hachiji dachi position, pivot counterclockwise on your right foot and step sharply back on your left into a right zenkutsu dachi stance facing enbusen line A. Simultaneously, block to the middle right (chudan block). However, as your left fist is pulled back in conjunction with the block, turn your palm toward the floor, not the ceiling, to begin preparation for a morote tsuki (double punch).

KATA NO. 35

Assume the morote tsuki (double punch) "ready" position by pulling your right hand back also, palm toward the ceiling. Keep your feet in the right zenkutsu dachi stance.

KATA NO. 36

Execute the morote tsuki, shooting your right hand toward your opponent's belt area, your left toward his heart. Your feet should not move out of their right zenkutsu dachi position.

BUNKAI NO. 34

A: Pivot counterclockwise on your left foot and step forward with your right into a right kihondachi stance facing B. As you step, execute a right chudan (middle) punch. B: Counter with a right chudan (middle) block. Simultaneously, pivot counterclockwise on your right foot and step back forty-five degrees with your left into a right zenkutsu dachi stance.

BUNKAI NOS. 35—36

B: Pivot counterclockwise on your right foot, step forward with your left into a left kihondachi stance and strike toward A with a left chudan (middle) punch. A: Pivot counterclockwise on your left foot, step back with your right into a left zenkutsu dachi stance and counter with a left chudan (middle) block.

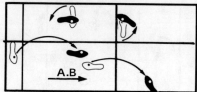

35

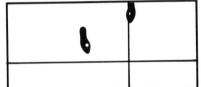

36

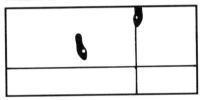

35-36

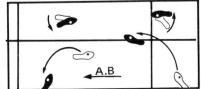

KATA NO. 37

From the zenkutsu dachi position, bring your left foot forward into a heikodachi stance with your heels parallel to enbusen line CD. Do not stand completely erect but keep your knees slightly bent with a little spring in them. Keep your arms extended as at the end of the morote tsuki.

KATA NO. 38

Step back in the direction of enbusen line B with your right foot and assume a left zenkutsu dachi stance. Block again, this time to the middle left (chudan block). When your right fist is pulled back in conjunction with the block, turn your palm toward the floor, not the ceiling, to begin preparation for a second morote tsuki (double punch).

KATA NO. 39

Pull your left hand, palm toward the ceiling, back into the morote tsuki "ready" position. Maintain the left zenkutsu dachi stance.

37

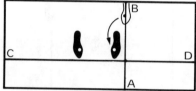

BUNKAI NOS. 37—38

A: Execute another right chudan (middle) punch. As you strike, move out of the zenkutsu dachi stance by pivoting clockwise on your left foot and stepping forward with your right into a right kihondachi stance. **B:** Counter A's movements by putting up a right chudan (middle) block and stepping back forty-five degrees with your left into a right zenkutsu dachi stance. Pivot clockwise slightly on your right foot as your left comes back.

BUNKAI NO. 39

B: Bring your right hand out of the chudan block and assume the morote tsuki (double punch) "ready" position. With both hands pulled back, make sure the palm of your left fist is turned toward the floor, the palm of your right toward the ceiling. **A:** Maintain your position—that is, hands as they were at the end of the right chudan punch (right arm extended, left fist withdrawn), feet in a right kihondachi stance.

37-38

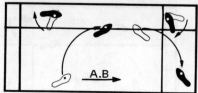

KATA NO. 40

Execute the blow. In this second double punch, use your right hand to hit toward the level of your opponent's heart; use your left to strike toward the area of and around his belt. Do not move out of the zenkutsu dachi stance or drop your hands after the attack has been completed.

KATA NO. 41

Begin the ending formality by bringing your hands from the completed morote tsuki into the closing position over your chest.

KATA NO. 42

Pivot counterclockwise on your left foot and step forward with your right into a musubi-dachi stance. Lower your hands into the "ready" position.

40

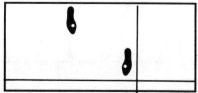

BUNKAI NO. 40

B: Complete the morote tsuki, striking out for the level of **A**'s heart with your left hand, the level of his belt with your right. **A:** Remain in place.

BUNKAI NO. 41

Begin the ending formality.
A: Bring your hands together to the closing position. Step back with your right foot and pivot counterclockwise on your left into a musubidachi stance. **B:** Move out of the zenkutsu dachi position, stepping back on your right foot as you bring your left toward it in the musubidachi stance. Bring your hands over your chest in the closing position.

BUNKAI NO. 42

Both **A** and **B**:
Lower your hands to the "ready" position.

40

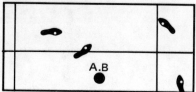

A.B

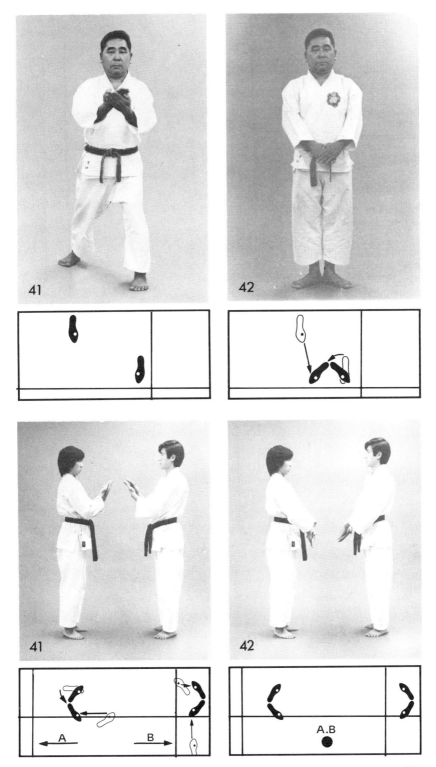

KATA NOS. 43-45
Complete the kata with the ending formality sequence of (43) attention, (44) bowing and (45) a return to attention.

43

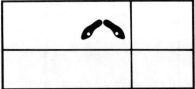

BUNKAI NOS. 43-45
Both **A** and **B:**
Complete the bunkai with the ending formality sequence of (43) attention, (44) bowing and (45) a return to attention.

43

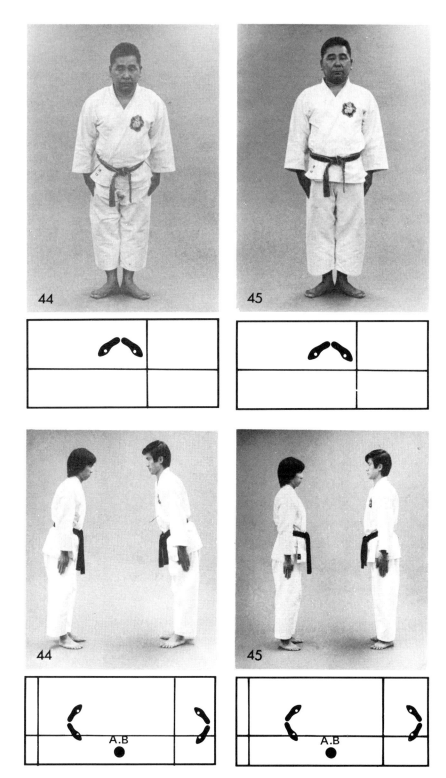

SANCHIN

Mastery of Okinawan Goju-Ryu Karate-Do hinges on an understanding of Sanchin training methods. For the advanced student, this means exploration of several technical elements. For the beginner, however, it means coordinating proper breathing with proper execution of techniques on all grade levels.

ZEN AND SANCHIN

The Japanese martial arts have always been deeply related to Buddhism and, in particular, Zen Buddhism. In essence, the ultimate goal of the serious martial artist, "reaching a stage of enlightenment," is rooted in Buddhism. Although others exist, two of the roads to this Buddhist "enlightenment" are the practice of "sitting Zen" and "standing Zen." While "sitting Zen" is based on stillness, "standing Zen" is based on action. Both, however, are one internal reality viewed and practiced from different perspectives.

In this discussion, the primary concern is the use of "standing Zen" in training. Both Zen monks in China's Shorin Temple and swordsmen in early Japan used "standing Zen" to help discipline, control and strengthen their physical and mental energies. Eventually, this "standing Zen" system of focusing energy on attaining a "stage of enlightenment" (and physical superiority) was developed into a method of martial arts training known as *Sanchin*.

Although every Japanese martial art style has its own individual characteristics, their origins can be traced to one source, a source that utilized this particular method of training. Therefore, it might be said that Sanchin was performed by all past styles. Looking at present-day karate, then, it seems strange that every style does not practice a perfect body training method such as Sanchin. (NOTE: In actuality, the physical education curriculums of some Okinawan schools practicing the Shorin style of karate did include Sanchin. However, because Sanchin was not suitable, medically speaking, for youths at the crucial stage of incipient manhood, it was later eliminated.)

It might prove helpful for students to look back once again and use the Sanchin methods and techniques of the past that still have value.

We can be proud of Sanchin. It is unique to karate and does not exist in any other Japanese martial art. I feel that it should be regarded not only as part of the Goju-Ryu system but as a precious resource of Okinawan Karate-Do.

Anyone who studies Goju-Ryu must first use Sanchin to develop proper breathing methods, basic body strength and mental power. The phrase, "Three-Year Sanchin," was heard often at our training sessions, with Sanchin accompanied by preparatory, complementary and utilitarian exercises used to develop body strength. After that, Sanchin training concentrated on open hand and combat practice forms.

Recently, karate has been studied with an emphasis on free-fighting without basic body training or prior training in basic techniques. This practice contradicts the essential aims of karate and can lead to both injuries and lifetime regrets. We must be careful.

Sanchin training is very difficult and complex. As a result, it cannot be explained here completely. Its use, however, is not exclusively limited to martial arts preparation. It does not necessitate much time or space. And, it can serve as a refreshing, physically beneficial diversion from study or work. Also, because it does not demand much in the way of either time or space, it can and should be practiced frequently.

SANCHIN TRAINING METHOD

While engaged in Sanchin training, observe the following:

(1) Maintain a correct posture.
(2) Coordinate proper breathing with correct techniques.
(3) Because the mind naturally tends toward laziness, actively keep it stimulated and alive.
(4) Always train both body and mind with affection.
(5) When striking a student's body, do so with reason, using force suitable to the student's rate of progress.Excessive force will upset his all-important posture.
(6) Strike a student's body while his breath is being held.
(7) Think about the harmony of strength and breathing so that there is no loosening of the body.
(8) Put sufficient strength in your lower abdomen.

SANCHIN WALKING

Sanchin walking and kihondachi walking (basic walking) are executed in exactly the same manner. That is, each step consists of two movements—A) stepping (either forward or backward) with the toes of both feet pointed inward/heels outward and B) turning on the balls of both feet to bring your heels inward and your hips upward (see section on kihondachi or basic walking for a more detailed explanation). Remember to bend your knees inward a little.

Please note that in the diagrams of Sanchin walking, the second movement of each step has not been drawn.

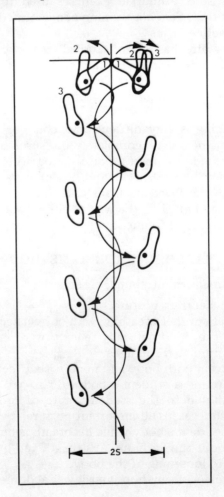

SANCHIN WALKING

1

2

3

THE FIVE TECHNIQUES in the BREATHING METHOD

During execution of open hand forms, combat practice forms, matches and other activities, consider three important technical factors:

(1) breathing

(2) movement of center of gravity

(3) variation of techniques

Only breathing will be discussed here. The other two factors will be covered at a future time.

Proper breathing is of the utmost importance whether one trains in the martial arts, the performing arts or athletics. Sanchin has its own unique, but nonetheless effective, method of breathing. Its value can be seen most clearly in a martial arts struggle where the ramifications of improper breathing can cost a fighter the match.

The Sanchin method of breathing may be broken down as follows:

(1) long inhale, long exhale

(2) long inhale, short exhale

(3) short inhale, long exhale

(4) short inhale, short exhale

(5) hold breath—inhale and hold, exhale and hold

Breathing exercises should be performed slowly and calmly, without forcing any movements. Also, it is important to remember to inhale through the nose and exhale through the mouth. The student should use the sounds of inhaling and exhaling to coordinate his breathing with his physical executions. The mind will then focus itself and concentrate quite naturally.

The following exercise consists of movements executed in conjunction with Sanchin breathing methods. Proper breathing techniques for each movement have been indicated with these symbols:

SYMBOLS for SANCHIN BREATHING

1. Long inhale ╱   Short inhale ↗

2. Long exhale ╲   Short exhale ↘

3. *Tai* — (Holding breath in lower abdomen)

   ● Strong   ○ Weak

4. *Jusoku* (Soft breathing—exhale without holding breath after inhaling)

   a. Long inhale and short exhale ╱↘

   b. Short inhale and long exhale ↗╲

   c. Long inhale and long exhale ╱╲

   d. Short inhale and short exhale ↗↘

5. *Taisoku*

   a. Hold breath after inhaling ○╱ ●╱

   b. Hold breath after exhaling ╲↓○ ╲●

IMPORTANT:
   INHALE THROUGH NOSE

   EXHALE THROUGH MOUTH

CLARIFICATION OF TECHNIQUES USED IN NOS. 6—46

Movements Nos. 6-46 are comprised primarily of chudan blocks, chudan punches and Sanchin walking. This side view sequence of these movements should help explain more clearly the basics involved. Compare these to the full face photographs presented in the actual exercise.

(1) Execute a chudan (middle) block with both arms—a sort of double chudan block. (2) Execute a left (or right, as the case may be) chudan (middle) block. In either instance, bring the fist not engaged in blocking to the side of your chest, palm up, as you pull your elbow down and back.

Simultaneously, inhale slowly through your nose. Do not force holding your breath but let it occur naturally and smoothly. (3) Keeping your blocking fist stationary, thrust your other one (whether right or left) out in a chudan (middle) punch on a level even with your solar plexus. Slowly and strongly, exhale through your mouth. Coordinate your breathing with the movement. That is, exhale as your striking fist turns over during execution of the punch. (4) Bring your hand out of the right or left punch into a chudan (middle) block with both arms.

CLARIFICATION OF TECHNIQUES USED IN NOS. 47—54

The exercise, from Nos. 47-54, consists of coordinating a push/pull motion of the arms with Sanchin breathing techniques. Here, too, it would be helpful to compare this side view sequence with the full face photographs in the actual exercise.

(1) Enter a chudan (middle) block with both arms. With a short intake of breath, quickly open your hands, palms facing the ceiling. Keep your thumbs bent in. (2) Push your hands forward, down and to the inside to a level even with your solar plexus. As you do so, twist your forearms inward so that the palms of your hands end facing the floor.

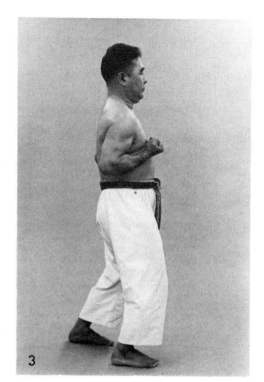

Bend your elbows slightly so that your arms form a rough circle. Do not let your elbows drop and remember to keep your hands open, thumbs bent in. Simultaneously, exhale slowly and hold your breath. (3) Pull both hands to the sides of your chest, slowly making fists as you turn your palms toward the ceiling. Keep your elbows down. At the same time, inhale slowly and hold. (4) Exhale slowly as you push your hands forward again, resuming the position of No. 2, that is, arms out on a level even with your solar plexus, hands open, palms toward the floor, elbows bent so that your arms form a rough circle.

SANCHIN EXERCISE

Unless otherwise indicated, the movements of the Sanchin exercise have been described in these terms:

    a. hand technique
    b. foot stance
    c. type of breathing

Also, because moving from one basic technique to another should now be self-explanatory, explicit directions will not be given. In addition, please note that unless otherwise specified, all blocks and punches are "chudan."

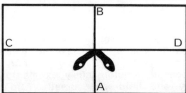

1. a. attention
   b. musubidachi
   c. normal breathing
2. a. bowing
   b. musubidachi
   c. normal breathing
3. a. attention
   b. musubidachi
   c. normal breathing
4. a. ready
   b. musubidachi
   c. long inhale, weak hold
5. a. opening
   b. heikodachi
   c. long exhale, strong hold
6. a. double block
   b. right kihondachi
   c. long inhale, short exhale, strong hold

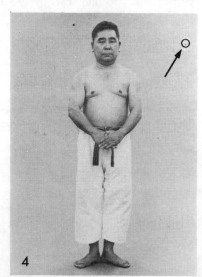

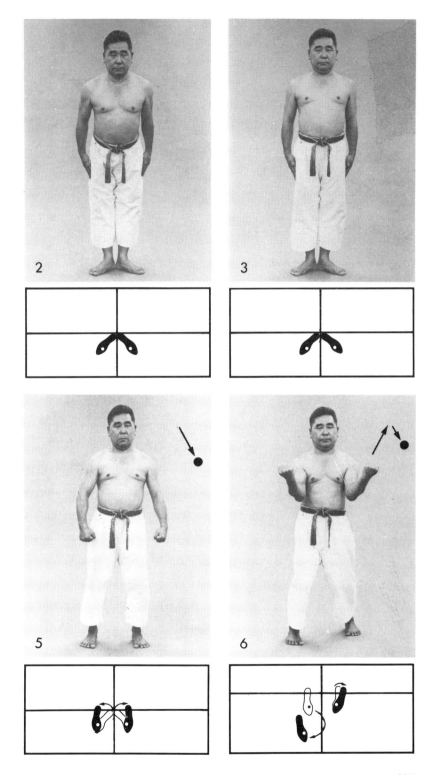

7. a. right block
   b. right kihondachi
   c. long inhale, weak hold
8. a. left punch
   b. right kihondachi
   c. long exhale, strong hold
9. a. double block
   b. right kihondachi
   c. long inhale, short exhale, strong hold

7

10. a. double block
    b. left kihondachi
    c. strong hold
11. a. left block
    b. left kihondachi
    c. long inhale, weak hold
12. a. right punch
    b. left kihondachi
    c. long exhale, strong hold

10

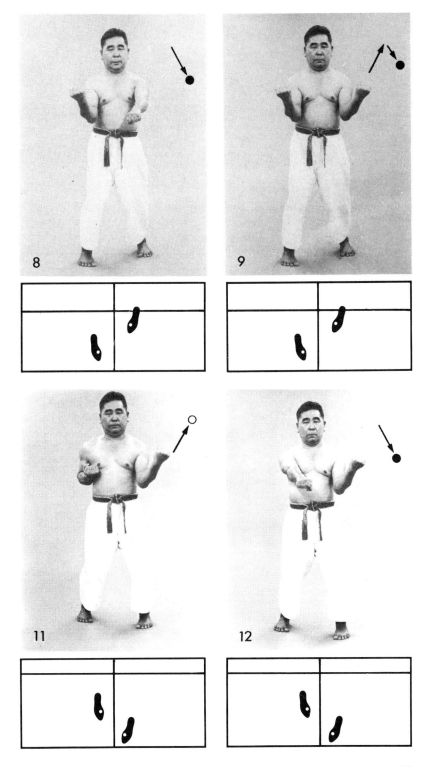

13 a. double block
   b. left kihondachi
   c. long inhale, short exhale,
      strong hold
14. a. double block
   b. right kihondachi
   c. strong hold
15. a. right block
   b. right kihondachi
   c. long inhale, weak hold

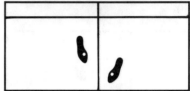

16. a. left punch
   b. right kihondachi
   c. long exhale, strong hold
17. a. right block
   b. right kihondachi
   c. long inhale, weak hold
18. a. Keep your right arm in the right block. Bending your left elbow, hold your left arm in front of you against your solar plexus. Position your left fist, palm toward the ceiling, between your right elbow and your torso. b. From the right kihondachi stance, pivot slightly counterclockwise on your left foot. Bring your right directly in front of it with a distance of 1.5 S between your left heel and the ball of your right foot (your feet should be parallel to enbusen line AD). Raise your right heel off the ground and bend both knees slightly. c. Short exhale, weak hold.

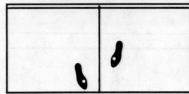

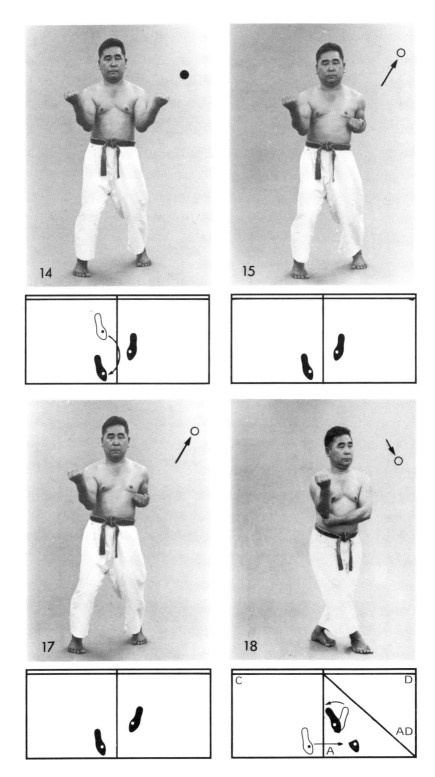

19. a. left block
    b. Pivot counterclockwise again, turning in the direction of enbusen line B into a left kihondachi.
    c. long inhale, weak hold
20. a. right punch
    b. left kihondachi
    c. long exhale, strong hold
21. a. double block
    b. left kihondachi
    c. long inhale, short exhale, strong hold

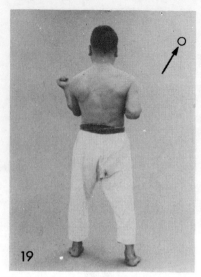

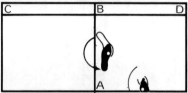

22. a. double block
    b. right kihondachi
    c. strong hold
23. a. right block
    b. right kihondachi
    c. long inhale, weak hold
24. a. left punch
    b. right kihondachi
    c. long exhale, strong hold

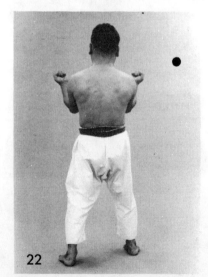

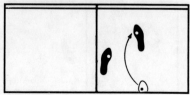

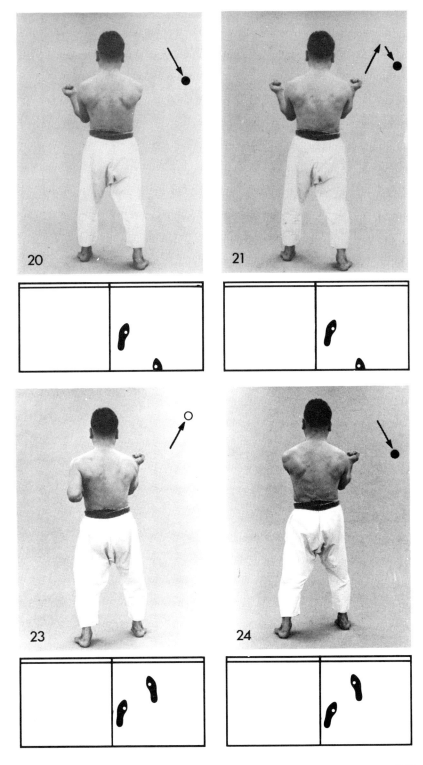

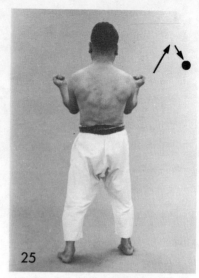

25. a. double block
    b. right kihondachi
    c. long inhale, short exhale, strong hold
26. a. double block
    b. left kihondachi
    c. strong hold
27. a. left block
    b. left kihondachi
    c. long inhale, weak hold

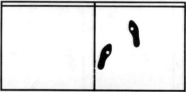

25

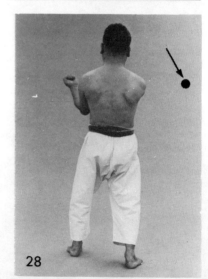

28. a. right punch
    b. left kihondachi
    c. long exhale, strong hold
29. a. double block
    b. left kihondachi
    c. long inhale, short exhale, strong hold
30. a. double block
    b. right kihondachi
    c. strong hold

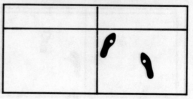

28

178

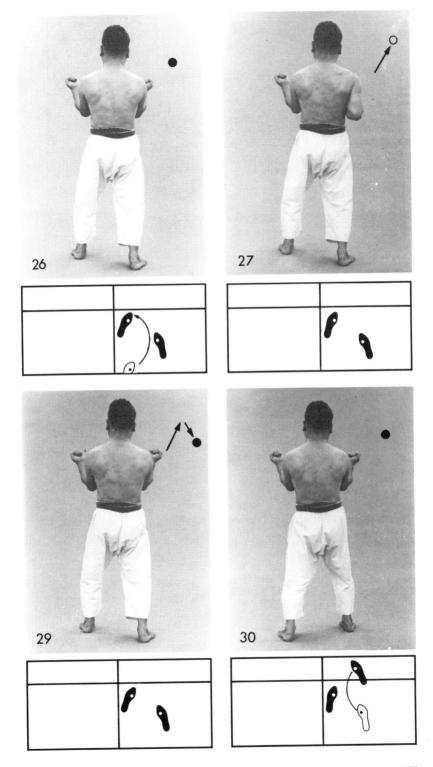

31

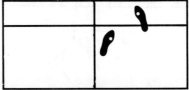

31. a. right block
    b. right kihondachi
    c. long inhale, weak hold
32. a. left punch
    b. right kihondachi
    c. long exhale, strong hold
33. a. right block
    b. right kihondachi
    c. long inhale, weak hold

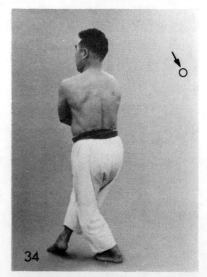

34

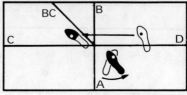

34. a. Keep your right arm in the right block. Bending your left elbow, hold your left arm in front of you against your solar plexus. Position your left fist, palm toward the ceiling, between your right elbow and your torso. b. Pivot slightly counterclockwise on your left foot. Bring your right directly in front of it with a distance of 1.5 S between your left heel and the ball of your right foot (your feet should be parallel to enbusen line BC). Raise your right heel off the ground and bend both knees slightly. c. Short exhale, weak hold.
35. a. left block
    b. pivot counterclockwise again, turning in the direction of enbusen line A into a left kihondachi
    c. long inhale, weak hold
36. a. right punch
    b. left kihondachi
    c. long exhale, strong hold

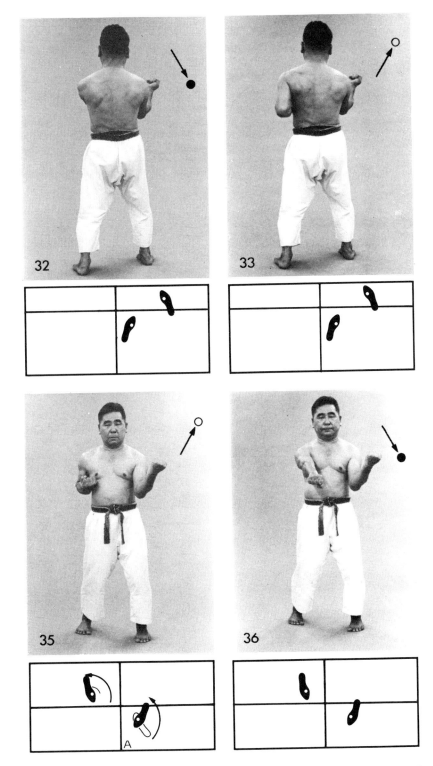

37. a. double block
    b. left kihondachi
    c. long inhale, short exhale, strong hold
38. a. double block
    b. right kihondachi
    c. strong hold
39. a. right block
    b. right kihondachi
    c. long inhale, weak hold

37

40. a. left punch
    b. right kihondachi
    c. long exhale, strong hold
41. a. double block
    b. right kihondachi
    c. long inhale, short exhale, strong hold
42. a. left block
    b. right kihondachi
    c. long inhale, weak hold

40

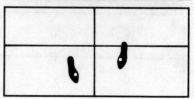

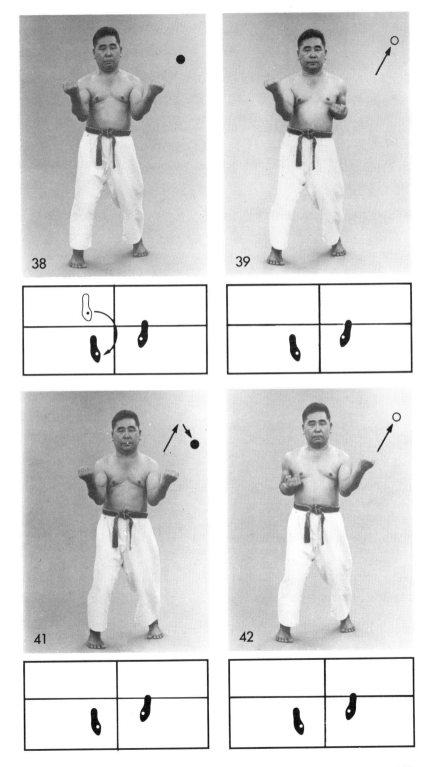

43. a. right punch
    b. right kihondachi
    c. long exhale, strong hold
44. a. double block
    b. right kihondachi
    c. long inhale, short exhale, strong hold
45. a. right block
    b. right kihondachi
    c. long inhale, weak hold

43

46. a. left punch
    b. right kihondachi
    c. long exhale, strong hold
47. a. pull both hands up, open with palms toward the ceiling.
    b. right kihondachi
    c. short inhale
48. a. push both hands out, open with palms toward the floor.
    b. right kihondachi
    c. long exhale, strong hold

46

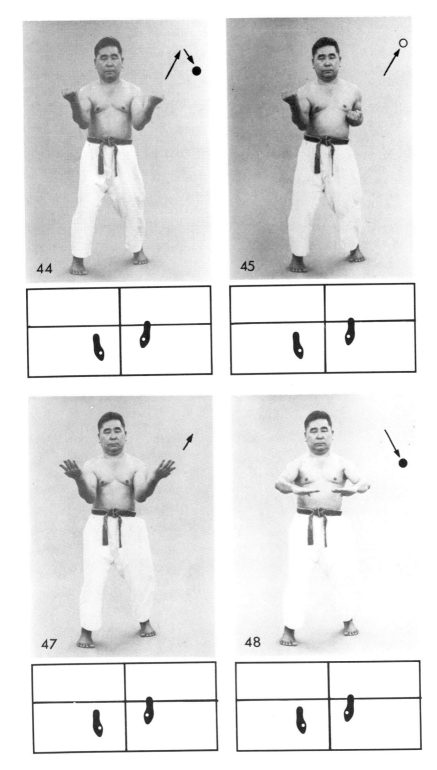

49. a. pull both hands back, fists clenched, palms toward the ceiling
    b. right kihondachi
    c. long inhale, weak hold
50. a. push both hands out, open with palms toward the floor
    b. right kihondachi
    c. long exhale, strong hold
51. a. pull both hands back, fists clenched, palms toward the ceiling
    b. right kihondachi
    c. long inhale, weak hold

49

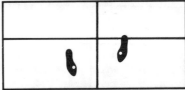

52. a. push both hands out, open with palms toward the floor
    b. right kihondachi
    c. long exhale, strong hold
53. a. pull both hands back, fists clenched, palms toward the ceiling
    b. right kihondachi
    c. long inhale, weak hold
54. a. push both hands out, open with palms toward the floor
    b. right kihondachi
    c. long exhale, strong hold

52

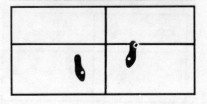

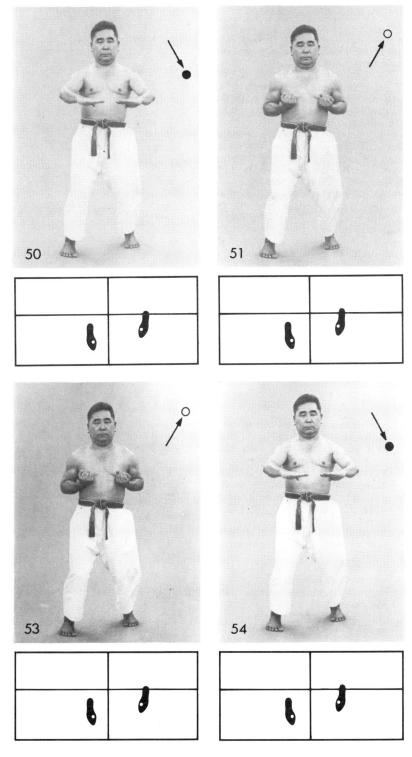

In reality, frames 55 through 57 should be executed in one smooth movement, with one breath.

55. a. Pull your right hand, open with palm toward the ceiling, to the chudan block position. Bending your left elbow, hold your left arm in front of you against your solar plexus. Place your open left hand, palm toward the floor, between your right elbow and your torso. b. Left kihondachi. c. Long inhale.

56. a. Keep your left arm stationary but pull your right elbow straight back so that your right hand comes down, open with palm toward the ceiling, on top of your left. b. Left kihondachi. c. Long inhale.

57. a. Circle your left arm back against your left side, elbow in a rough 90 degree angle, wrist bent backwards, hand open with palm facing forward, fingers to the floor. Keep your right arm in place. b. Left kihondachi. c. Long inhale.

55

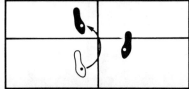

58. a. Bring your half open right hand forward and up to a level directly in front of and even with your right shoulder. As you do so, twist your wrist and bend it backwards so that your palm is to the front. Extend your left hand, straightening your elbow, on a level even with your groin, keeping it open, palm forward, wrist straight. b. Left kihondachi. c. Long exhale, strong hold.

59. a. closing
    b. musubidachi
    c. long inhale, weak hold

60. a. ready
    b. musubidachi
    c. 1) long exhale, weak hold
       2) short inhale, long exhale, weak hold
       3) short inhale, long exhale, weak hold
       4) short inhale, long exhale, weak hold

58

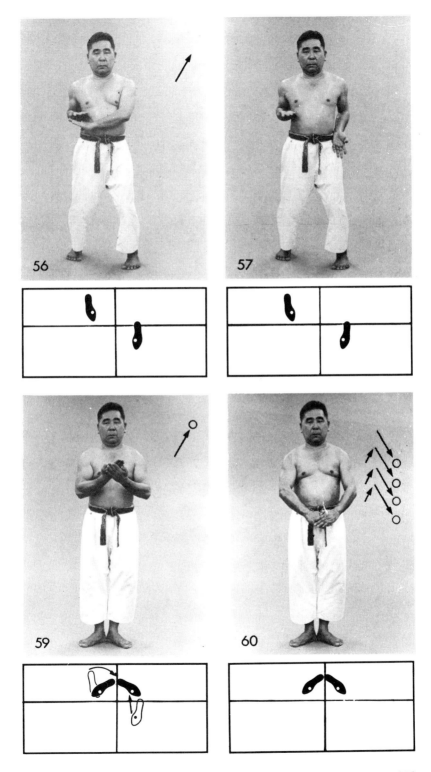

61. a. attention
    b. musubidachi
    c. normal breathing
62. a. bowing
    b. musubidachi
    c. normal breathing
63. a. attention
    b. musubidachi
    c. normal breathing

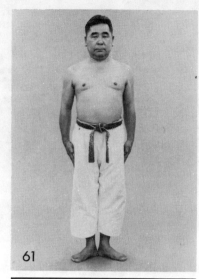

61

62

63

GLOSSARY

Basic Rules

Enbusen diagram — Kata's direction diagram
Sokucho — Foot length

Stance

Musubidachi — closed stance
Heikodachi — parallel stance
Kihondachi — basic stance (also called Sanchin dachi)
Zenkutsu dachi — forward stance
Sho zenkutsu dachi — small forward stance
Shikodachi — square or horse stance
Renoji dachi — V stance
Hachiji dachi — natural stance

Position

Kamae — basic on-guard position

Techniques

Seiken — regular karate fist
Jodan tsuki — high punch
Chudan tsuki — middle punch
Gedan tsuki — low punch
Jodan uke — high block
Chudan uke — middle block
Gedan uke — low block
Suihei shuto uchi — side chop strike
Morote tsuki — double hand punch
Yoko kentsui uchi — side hammer strike
Age tsuki — upper cut
Shomen geri — front kick
Tate empi — upward elbow strike
Uraken uchi — back fist strike
Mae shuto uchi — front chop strike
Soko tsuki — under cut